The Greatest Sales Book in the World

A Compilation of The Greatest Sales Presentations, Sales Scripts, Telemarketing Scripts, Rebuttals, Mailers, Referral Scripts and Tracking and Projection Reports The World Has Ever Seen!

By

Oliver P. Maldonado

authorHOUSE·

AuthorHouse™
1663 Liberty Drive
Bloomington, IN 47403
www.authorhouse.com
Phone: 833-262-8899

Published by AuthorHouse 10/10/2025

ISBN: 978-1-4184-9806-1 (sc)
ISBN: 978-1-4685-1531-2 (e)

Print information available on the last page.

Any people depicted in stock imagery provided by Getty Images are models, and such images are being used for illustrative purposes only.
Certain stock imagery © Getty Images.

This book is printed on acid-free paper.

Because of the dynamic nature of the Internet, any web addresses or links contained in this book may have changed since publication and may no longer be valid. The views expressed in this work are solely those of the author and do not necessarily reflect the views of the publisher, and the publisher hereby disclaims any responsibility for them.

Dedication

As always I would like to dedicate this book to my Daughter Isabelle, My brothers Sean and Damian who have been in the Sales Industry for many years "Making Miracles Happen!" My younger brother Daniel who is about to embark on the great adventure of life, and my mother Zaida who has been one of the biggest inspirations in my life and continues to keep on keeping on!

I would also like to make a special dedication to all of the Salespeople around the World who get up each and every day to sell something to someone. I know it is all of you who truly make the world go round. Sometimes the business we have chosen might seem a little ruthless or the changing times and economy might interfere with our better judgment! But let me remind you that is why we got into sales to begin with! We wanted to control our own destiny and we are all lucky to have the opportunity to be able to control our own destinies! Even the most seasoned sales veterans sometimes need some motivating words, or some new points of view, new ideas or even just getting back to basics. For all of the Salespeople around the World, I'd like to share this poem with you which has comforted me for many years. From an unknown author:

Don't Quit
When things go wrong as they sometimes will,
When the road you're trudging seems all up hill,
When the funds are low and the debts are high,
And you want to smile, but you have to sigh,
When care is pressing you down a bit,
Rest if you must, but don't you quit!
Success is failure turned inside out,
The silver tint on the clouds of doubt,

And you never can tell how close you are,
It may be near when it seems afar;
So stick to the fight when you're hardest hit.
It's when things seem worst that you musn't quit!!

He Turned a Simple Recipe into $Millions!

Broke and alone and only having the strong desire to succeed and using the principals of The Greatest Salesbook in the World, Colonel Sanders went out and began door knocking and selling his recipe to restaurants and built an organization that in the year 2000 had an annual sales volume of $8.9 Billion Dollars.

When the Colonel first started out on his mission he didn't own a restaurant, he wasn't a young man, he didn't have an education he only had a strong desire to succeed. How could someone that didn't even own a restaurant be able to create the empire that he had created? Well he was one of the greatest salespeople in the world, but his desire to succeed was what made him. When he first went out meeting with restaurants and their owners he got rejected. He got rejected a lot, in fact he got rejected over 1,000 times before he got his first yes! Now I know many people would have given up by the 9th or 20th no! But that is what having a strong determination does, it gets you what you want!

When the Colonel first went out, he had this great recipe and he started visiting restaurants traveling around the country and he would promise the restaurants more profit than they had ever seen if they used his secret recipe. Most restaurants at the time were burger restaurants and he was not only persuading the restaurant owners to use his secret recipe but to change their entire restaurants menu, meaning this was a chicken recipe so the restaurant would have to switch from selling burgers to selling chicken.

The Colonel was right and all restaurants he serviced with his recipe did experience more success than they had experienced before.

He did this for many years and he had a lot of success. Without owning a single restaurant he had over 1,200 restaurant accounts that he provided his secret recipe for.

As you know, the Colonel also revolutionized the restaurant industry and created one of the most successful fast food restaurants in the world. Kentucky Fried Chicken has a unique product virtually unmatched today. There are many fast food restaurants, but not many fast food chicken restaurants.

The Colonel was one of the greatest salespeople in the world who used the words of the "The Greatest Salesbook in the World" along with The 10 Sales Commandments to take his sales ability to a level unseen before.

Table of Contents

Introduction

A Great Salespersons Story

As I sat in my office late one night, I began to think how successful and fortunate I am. I looked around myself at some of the materials I have acquired over the years that adorned my office. I picked up the 150 million year old dinosaur tooth that sat on a shelf and admired it. I remember how long I have wanted this tooth.

I then looked at the god of fortune statute that sat on the shelf next to the dinosaur tooth that I picked up while vacationing out of the country. I glanced out of my corner office window in the penthouse suite looking over the mountains and downtown. I then looked out at the lake where I kept my boat which was about a 7 minute drive from my office building. I then looked at the frame that held the pictures of my most prized possession! The very thing I was the most proud of in my entire life. It was pictures of my biggest success, my daughter Isabelle! I wasn't successful because of my material possessions or my big corner office, it was because of my beautiful daughter and she was one of the motivating factors that has helped me achieve.

It was a great evening and the sun was setting over the mountains. I looked back at my life and wanted to remember how I made it here. Wow, just a few years ago, I was working 3 jobs, one of which was cleaning office suites just 4 miles from where my office was.

I remembered sitting in other executive chairs while I cleaned their office thinking, someday I would love it if I had an office near as nice. I remember looking at the cubes of the sales staff thinking someday I'd like a cube like that when I get my career started. I cleaned the office of a large successful radio station, and I was rubbing shoulders with some of the top sales people in the state, and although at the time, I had already had a successful sales career traveling the country. They had no idea I was one of the best salespeople in the country and no one there knew of me. I was just the cleaning guy who came at 6pm and cleaned until 11pm.

I thought back at what I thought then, and how I got there. I remembered that was during one of my first failures. I had traveled the country starting new sales and marketing offices for other organizations. I was a national sales and marketing consultant and earned a great living, but also spent the money living the life of a young successful sales person. After years of selling on the road and putting in my dues, I earned a masters degree and doctorate in the school of hard knocks. I remember thinking, I had made several small fortunes and earned companies millions of dollars, and I was now an office cleaner. I remember living like a movie star. I traveled, stayed in fancy hotels, vacationed almost monthly, rubbed shoulders with the rich and famous!

I remembered when I sat in one of the corner offices that I cleaned and I looked back then also and tried to figure out how I had gotten to that point. After years and years of successful selling around the country, I was very well known as an expert in my industry. I was highly recruited and yet, I was working three jobs and cleaning offices trying to regain what I had lost.

I thought back at the sales and marketing consulting firm I had started after many successful years doing it for someone else. I remember how I had reached some level of success and how I put in more years earning a decent living enjoying an extravagant lifestyle most could only dream and wish for.

I sat there in that office, looking out of the window thinking to myself, wow! I have lived a great life, and although, I have lost it all! I was proud of myself in the fact that I would do anything to get it back. I didn't think for a second that I wouldn't earn it all back and then some. I knew I had no formal education, other than my masters and doctorates from the school of hard knocks. I remember thinking, after years of hard work, years of earning a great income, I had lost it all because of companies I had hired to manage my money. People in my organization I trusted that failed me. I was burnt out and had to recharge my batteries, but I couldn't do it with fun, vacations or even time off. I had to recharge my batteries by taking brainless jobs where I could work and use my brain to figure out what went wrong and what I needed to do to get it all back.

I then smiled and got back to work with a smile on my face. I remember smiling and thinking to myself, "it was all worth it"! I realized I had already lived a great adventure, and I was headed for another great adventure getting it all back. Although I was a veteran salesman and businessman who has been selling and in business for over 15 years, I remember laughing out loud and thinking, "What am I worried about, I have a lot of talent, and I'm only 22 years old"!

My name is Oliver P. Maldonado and this is my story.

I remember when I discovered sales. I was just a boy of about 7 years when I discovered sales. I remember I was sitting at my babysitters house and one day I remember my babysitter very happy and exited. She was talking with with her daughter and they mentioned how they were going to get a lot of money. I was curious how they were going to do that. I remember money was always an issue in my life. I was the son of a single parent. I remember always wishing I could help and wishing I had more money, so I was very interested in how they were going to get all this money they talked about. I remember other than babysitting, I didn't think they worked. And they were always home.

So I was paying close attention to what was to take place so I could see how they were going to get this money they spoke of.

Sure enough, just as they mentioned, people were coming over and giving them money and then they would also picked something up. I remember they had a closet full of merchandise. They had products such as perfumes, make up, cologne, lotions, etc. I thought it was great how they had people coming over and giving them money for this. At the time I was just a boy and didn't realize it, ut she was selling Avon. I wanted to ask them if I could do it. I wanted to be able to have products at my house and have people come over and drop money off to me and I'd give them the products. I thought to myself, I can do this!

So I asked my babysitter if I could help her. She asked how. I said, I can do this. If you can tell me where you get the merchandise, I'll have some ot my house and I'll have my neighbors give me money for it. My babysitter mentioned it's not that easy. I didn't understand, and she explained. How will you pay for the products? I didn't know I responded? I didn't know you had to pay for it. She also asked how will people know I had them? I responded, I didn't know, I just saw people come over to your house and I figured they'd come over mine too. She then told me, well as I said it's not that easy, but if you'd like, you can help me. I said okay what do I need to do. She said, the way she gets people to know she had products and things to sell is by distributing her Avon magazines. These magazines have her name and number on them and instructions on how to place orders and such. I said okay, I'll do it. I then began going around the neighborhood and distributed these magazines. I didn't understand it completely at the time how it would all work, but it made sense. I just wanted to see it work so I could learn more.

A few days later and sure enough, people started coming over with money and picking up things that they had bought. I was thinking this is too easy, and I wanted to do it also.

I went back to my babysitter and asked how I could do what she does? How can I distribute magazines and have people come to my house and give me money. She said if I helped her more and helped her not only with the distribution of her magazines, but also help her with taking orders, picking up and delivering the products to her clients, that she would pay me. She also said then I would learn what needs to be done. She asked where I would give out the magazines. I said I live in a high rise building and theres another building next to mine. My building had 22 stories and the building next to mine had 21. I didn't know how many people that was, but I knew I could distribute more magazines in my building than her neighborhood, and I also figured I would get more people to give me money since they only had to walk a little way to pick up their product.

I was very exited! I could do this. I also had already learned about getting people to give me the money faster by not waiting for them, but by delivering the products to them. If I made it to them, I could get money quicker. So I learned how to take and place orders, and soon after that, I began distributing magazines in my buildings. It was great.

I also learned knew things. I remember as I was delivering products, people began to notice me. They asked me questions and what I was doing and pretty soon, they started placing orders with me. I also remember leaning that even people that didn't place orders would offer me money for products I was carrying. I then began placing orders for myself and then selling them the same day.

I remember after doing this for awhile, I was getting some money here and there, but I do remember getting my first big money. I remember one week, my babysitter gave me $72 dollars! Wow, that was the most money I had ever had. Remember I was only 8 years old. I loved the feeling it gave me, and I remember thinking, I can't believe I had earned this money, it was so easy. I wanted more of it.

This was my introduction into the sales business! I knew I wanted more. We moved away and I didn't have any connections with Avon and couldn't distribute any magazines. But I had already learned and developed some skills. I knew I could go around to peoples doors and ask for a sale, and that if I did this enough times with enough people, I would be able to sell and make money. But now, I had no products and no magazines to distribute. I tried to figure out what to sell? I really didn't know and I was still only 8-9 years old. I asked several people what I could sell. Most said I shouldn't be thinking of those things and that I really couldn't be selling anything. I asked why, almost everyone told me it was because I was only 8-9 years old. I heard this a lot. I remember once asking the old man that always seemed very wise, and always had advice and time for the kids in the neighborhood. He was retired and had the biggest house on the street and also had the nicest everything. I asked the old man down the street if he knew what I could sell to people and if he also knew how I could get it?

The old man told me, well why is it you want to do this. I said well to make money. He looked at me with a smile on his face and he said, well if that's the reason, you really don't have to sell people something to make money. I didn't understand, if I didn't sell them something why would they give me money? He said well, you could do something for them? I asked what do you mean? The old man said, you can provide them a service. Service I asked, he said yes. The old man said, I've seen you mowing your lawn so I know you can mow lawn very well. You could mow peoples lawn and they would pay you for it. I asked why would people pay me for mowing there lawn when they can do it themselves. He said, because even though they can they would rather not. Some are also busy, and others would rather pay someone. I said I didn't understand? He said, I'll give you an example. I'm very busy today and will be leaving for the day. I need my lawn mowed, and I would be willing to pay you to do it. I said really? He said yes. I went to get my mower and was ready to mow his lawn. When I got back, I mowed his lawn, and he said why did you mow my lawn? I said because you said you'd pay me for it. The old man said, but I never told you how much? I then realized oh, what if he gives me less than the gas I used? He said, if I gave you a quarter would you have agreed to do it? I said no, because I would use more than a quarter of gasoline. He said, next time remember to ask how much someone is willing to pay you, or let them know how much you're charging to mow it.

I learned a good lesson that day and he gave me a $5 dollar bill!! Wow that was easy, I then felt great. I felt a great rush and wanted to do it again and wanted to make more money!

So then I started going door to door to see if I could get more people to pay me to mow their lawn.

I remember the first few doors I knocked on, there was no answers. Then I remember the first few people that answered their doors, and the majority said no. I also remember that I really didn't know what to say. I remember not being prepared to answer their questions. A few were rude to me. I didn't understand why?

So I realized it wasn't going to be as easy as I thought. I wanted to be prepared and I wanted to be able to say the right things and to answer their questions. So I began talking to myself in my mind. Picturing what I would say at the door. I could see myself with a big smile on my face and asking if I could mow their lawn. I saw it and I was feeling pretty good about it.

I remember even a few people that made me feel a little silly, but they were right. One person just pointed out the fact that they had just finished mowing their lawn and wished I would have made it to their house a few hours earlier. It never even crossed my mind to see if they had just mowed their lawn or even if their lawn needed mowing.

I looked back behind me to see the other homes I had knocked on their doors and to my surprise, a lot of them didn't look that bad. Most were okay and most weren't home. Now, I realized I could have saved myself a lot of time, had I just paid attention to the lawns. I just figured everyone needed their lawns mowed, but didn't realize that some had already done it themselves. I had wasted a lot of the day going to the wrong doors of people that wouldn't have paid me to mow their lawn since they had just done it, or even if they had just done it a day or two before.

So now I came up with a new plan of attach. I didn't just go to every door, I looked at the lawns that needed the mowing the worst. The ones that looked as if no one had touched it for a long time. And sure enough, the next day, I had done several lawns, in less time than what I had already spent the day before just going door to door. I was feeling pretty good again. After awhile, I had hit most people in my neighborhood, and had no transportation to go outside of my neighborhood. I tried to figure out how I could do more lawns. So I started asking people what I should do, or how I could get more business. I learned how to do flyers, which worked out great. I also learned how to prospect first, so that I could cover twice as much ground and after getting several people to say yes, to then do 2-3 or 4 lawns that I have pre-set up already. I even had a great idea from a business man that said, why don't you start setting something up with people you've already done before, and let them know that you'll give them a discount if they have you come twice a month or every week? That way their lawn would get more attention and at a cheaper rate so we both win. That also worked out pretty good.

I was doing alright as a kid earning extra money when I needed it, but one day, I saw a van at the end of the corner and there were a lot of young kids hanging around it. There were boxes on the floor and a lot of candy laying around. The kids were talking with the adults as if in a meeting style. Everyone was taking what I've come to learn as inventory. Some were asking for more candy, some for a specific type of candy. Others were stocking everything. I was very impressed with these kids. I hung around to see what was going on. After most of the kids had gone, I asked the adults what was going on. I already knew that I've seen these kids going door to door selling candy, and I wanted in on it.

So he explained the situation to me, and told me that he takes the kids to the different neighborhoods and lets them sell candy door to door. He said they drive to all kinds of neighborhoods. That's what I wanted to do, go to other neighborhoods and sell door to door. I knew I could do it if I just had something to sell.

The man told me that I could make $60-$80-$100 plus dollars per week. Wow! That's more than I was making doing lawns, and I would be able to talk with everyone.

To make a long story short on the candy selling, it was a scam and although I sold a lot, most of the money was kept by the guys running the show. They set high prices and said I could keep everything above and beyond what I collect. The problem was that I didn't want to overcharge what I thought was unreasonable and also I didn't want to loose and not outsell everyone. It was a good experience for me as far as work went, but that was about it.

I also remembered that they had actual scripts and presentations that they did. I loved that.

Wow, as I looked back at my child hood, all I can remember was all I ever wantcd to do was sell!

I looked around my office and then also saw my brief case! I remember when I was 10 years old, all I wanted for my birthday and Christmas was a business briefcase. I told my mother and grandparents. I remember they all kept asking me if I was serious. If I didn't want some toys? Why did I want a briefcase? I was only 10 years old? Yes! I would always reply. I wanted one, it was the thing I wanted the most. I can't remember anyting I ever wanted more.

So my birthday came and I didn't get a briefcase. Everyone was surprised when I looked a little disspointed. I was appreciative of my gifts, but I really did want a briefcase. I think they realized it, and they asked me again. I said yes, and they said I was too young and wouldn't be able to use ot for anything.

So Christmas came around and I opened all of my gifts and no briefcase. I was disappointed and then my mother and grandmother said there was one more gift for me they forgot about. It was a box, I remember it well. It looked as if it were a briefcase size! Could it be?

I grabbed it and opened it, and sure enough there it sat a business briefcase! I was so exited!!! I couldn't believe it, I got a business briefcase! It looked great! It had the folders inside so I could put documents and files. It had space for my pens and pencils, it was great! I loved it. I remember taking it to school with me. Although I got funny looks, no one really teased me. I was no wimp you see! I eventually stoped taking my briefcase with me. It wasn't meant for a kid to go to school with. Not easy to maneuver and walk around with or even carry.

As far back as I could remember I always wanted to be a Salesman!

The Ten Sales Commandments

The 1ˢᵗ Sales Commandment

Today I've decided to start a new life.

The only thing I can control in this world is me and today I've decided to start a new life and leave my old life behind. In my old life I suffered, struggled and failed for too long. If I continued down the path of my old life, I would have been doomed to live a life of mediocrity, struggle, and misery.

Today I decide to start a new life.

Today I will start a new life where everything is possible. Today I've realized that the career I have chosen is paved with gold and riches beyond my wildest dreams and there is nothing but opportunity awaiting me and I will succeed. Today I have realized that I have failed in the past and there will be many more people who will fail in front of me like doomed men giving up creating large piles of doomed souls in front of me which will not have any affect on me, and I will not fail like the others for I have already failed for too long and today I decide to start a new life.

I've put in my dues and already given years of struggle and failure and I will no longer accept that as my reality. Failure will now be foreign to me and I will no longer tolerate or accept struggle as payment for success. Now I will reject failure and I am prepared to accept success as my payment for my past struggles. I will use what I've learned over the years and what I will learn from this book and I demand everything that is due to me in full and with interest. My time is now and I will only accept success, wealth and happiness beyond my wildest dreams as payment in full.

Today I decided to start a new life and my determination to succeed is strong enough to get me there. I will not fail and I will use everything in my power to reach a level of wealth, success and happiness larger than I had even imagined it in my dreams.

Today I decided to start a new life and I know no matter what happens, good or bad what an adventure it will be.

Today I decided to start a new life!

The 2ⁿᵈ Sales Commandment

I will start each day by being positive and having a great attitude.

I have begun a new life and in this new life, I will be positive with a great attitude. In order for me to succeed and acquire the riches and happiness that is due me in my new life, I must always be amazingly positive and exude a great attitude.

I will receive and I expect resistance from others regarding my new positive and great attitude, but I know that neither my co-workers nor prospects nor close relatives will be able to resist my contagious positive and great attitude.

I am exited to have come to this defining moment and I have accepted the challenge to make all of my wildest dreams a reality by starting each day by being positive and having a great attitude.

I will start each day by being positive and having a great attitude since I am on the doorsteps of greatness. My time is now and there is absolutely no reason why not to feel and be positive with a great attitude since I am well on my way to reaching all of my dreams. Why would someone destined for greatness be anything less than positive with a great attitude? Someone destined for greatness would never be anything less than positive with a great attitude and since I am also destined for greatness and amazing success I will start each day by doing the same and being positive with a great attitude.

Today is going to be a great day!

I will face today and everyday knowing that it will be a great day since I am the master of each day and how the day plays out I will make today and every day that follows a great day.

I will make today and everyday forward a great day. I and only I alone can control my emotions and feelings and I am also the master of my days and I will make it a great day for today is the only day I can make great at this very moment therefore the only day I can and will make great is today.

I will start each day by being positive and having a great attitude and I will infect anyone and everyone who near me with my positive thinking and great attitude!

The 3rd Sales Commandment

I will not give up and I will persist until I accomplish and reach my goals.

Although I will encounter many obstacles in my path to greatness and the world will try to stop me. I will not allow them to deter me. I will not give up. I know that these obstacles I will face will be more than many men or women can handle yet they will not deter me for even a millionth of a second. No matter what dragons I will have to face and encounter, I am a dragon slayer and I will persist until I have slain each and every dragon that dares to test my will and I will persist until I accomplish and reach my goals. I will never quit because I don't know what that word means. I will not acknowledge such a word unless they are my goals who realize that it is inevitable and it will be my goals who quit making me chase them since they have realized they are being chased by the worlds most persistent human being that has ever lived.

I will persist until I accomplish and reach my goals.

I will not quit and when I need motivation I will refer to this motivating poem by an unknown poet. This poem is refreshing and although I do not know who wrote the poem I know it must have been written by someone who has also persisted and has reached their goals. I know the person who wrote this very powerful poem has seen their own share of dragons and was successful in slaying all dragons who appeared before them and like them I will do the same and in a time of weakness, I will look to this poem and find the needed strength that will help me accomplish and reach my goals.

Don't Quit
When things go wrong as they sometimes will,
When the road you're trudging seems all up hill,
When the funds are low and the debts are high,

And you want to smile, but you have to sigh,
When care is pressing you down a bit,
Rest if you must, but don't you quit!
Success is failure turned inside out,
The silver tint on the clouds of doubt,
And you never can tell how close you are,
It may be near when it seems afar;
So stick to the fight when you're hardest hit.
It's when things seem worst that you musn't quit!!

The 4th Sales Commandment

I must create lasting change in my life.

I have realized that what I have been doing has not worked for me. If I continue doing the things that have not worked, I will fail. I will not succeed. I will be considered a failure, a looser. If I do not change I will suffer and feel immediate, unbearable and devastating amounts of pain, so I must change.
I must create lasting change in my life.

I have already been told by my friends, family and the world that I cannot change. That I cannot achieve. I am well aware that they have become numb by their own past failures. I know they have been brain washed by society and they have also been conditioned to what they cannot do. I will not follow in their footsteps and allow them to attempt to brain wash me. I will not become numb to their voices and words of failure. I will not allow them to speak such nonsense around me and tell me what they think I cannot do. When anyone including my family, friends, co-workers and acquaintances try to convince me on the things I cannot do, I will correct them and tell them I can, will and must change things in my life to achieve all of my goals in life.
I must create lasting change in my life.
I will feed from my successes. Small successes in the beginning will be just enough nourishment to keep me from starving, but the effects have triggered a reaction I will not be able to control. The changes I will have made in my life have triggered these senses within me that are uncontrollable. I will have become addicted to the sensation of my successes that are now stacking atop each other. Each success makes me stronger than the last. With each success, my hunger for more success grows and grows. I will feed from my successes which I will need in order to survive. The lasting changes I have made in my life will bring me more material things and finances which have made my family, friends and acquaintances

believe in me. Now they are also making changes in their lives to try and follow my footsteps. I must create lasting change in my life so I can not only help myself but also the people I care about the most which will also bring me the most amount of happiness and pleasure that will help feed my appetite.

I must create lasting change in my life.

The 5th Sales Commandment

I will live today to the Fullest!

On this day I choose to live it to the fullest I can possibly live it. Since I will live this day to the fullest, I will have no time to waste on worrying about my past failures. I have learned from my failures and I appreciate the lessons I have learned from them. My past failures have made me a stronger, better wiser salesperson so I will live today to the fullest and have the assurance that my past failures were necessary to get me to this day which is a step closer to reaching all my goals and dreams. For that I am grateful and I will live today to the fullest.

I will not worry about tomorrow. I cannot live today to the fullest and achieve everything I must and reach my goals today if I have the worry about tomorrow clouding my judgment today. Therefore I will not worry about tomorrow today. In order for me to reach tomorrow I must finish out today and today I will live to the fullest. Since I will live today to the fullest and achieve my goals today, I know that my actions today will better tomorrow. With the confidence and knowledge of knowing my actions today will better tomorrow, I will not worry about tomorrow.

I will live today to the fullest.

The only thing I can control in this world is myself and what I do today. I will live today to the fullest and reach my goals which will make all of my dreams come true.

I will live today to the fullest.

The 6ᵗʰ Sales Commandment

I will control my emotions everyday.

I cannot control many things in life. Things are constantly changing in my world. People come and go, acquaintances fade, the seasons change, children grow up, economies change, and the world around me will continue to change forever. I cannot control many things in the world around me except myself. The only thing I can control in this world is me and how I feel and I will control my emotions everyday.

Emotions are merely definitions each individual person gives to how they are feeling. Emotions are not planted in me, other than the definition I give it myself. When a difficult or bad situation arises in my life, I can feel to get frustrated or mad or I can merely look at it as a challenge and control my emotions to find a more productive way to meet the challenge before me. Either way I look at it, the situation itself will remain the self regardless of which emotion I choose to feel. I am the master of my emotions and which emotion I choose to feel is up to me and only me and I will control my emotions everyday. There are emotions that can empower me and emotions that can disempower me and I will control my emotions everyday and choose the emotions that will empower me to overcome anything I will encounter each day. I choose to be wise and select the emotion that will empower me which will help me in each situation I encounter. Sometimes I may select to be happy while other times I may need to feel determined to accomplish a task. No matter what emotions I feel whether it be happy, determined, persistent, energetic or even peeved sometimes

I will control my emotions everyday and select the emption that will empower me. In situations when a negative emotion has caught me by surprise I will know immediately that is not the most optimum emotion and I since I am the only one who can control my emotions I will select a better empowering emotion.

I am the master of my emotions and I will control my emotions everyday!

The 7ᵗʰ Sales Commandment

I will live my life as a happy energetic person.

Happy energetic people have the most friends and fun than everyone else. In actuality happy energetic people have the most of everything. They have more friends because most people want to be around someone that is happy and energetic. Even people they do not know are constantly attracted to them always approaching them to speak with them whether in an elevator, convention or park, happy energetic people are contagious and always attract others to them, so they are constantly making new friends. I will live my life as a happy energetic person. They have the greatest relationships business and personal. Happy energetic people have the most business and clientele because they attract other people who want to be around them and work with them, so like them I will live life as a happy energetic person. Since I will live my life as a happy energetic person I will have the most friends and that will make me a happier person. By being happy and energetic I will also start making friends with new business associates and I will also start acquiring more and more clients and my clients will then refer me to more prospects since they will want their friends and family to be around someone as happy and energetic like me.

I will live my life as a happy energetic person.

There is much more to living my life as a happy energetic person than just making new friends, having more relationships and clients. I will also be able to affect and influence in a positive way all of the people I care about the most. My loved ones will benefit from my new happy energetic personality and I will be able to brighten their lives which in turn will brighten my life even more. My new contagious happy energetic personality will soon rub off on them and they too will live happier more energetic lives and that will affect their other loved ones and their relationships.

I will live my life as a happy energetic person.

Although there will be challenging times ahead, I will live my life as a happy energetic person and which will help overcome the challenges I am sure to face in the future.

Living as a happy energetic person will be a way of life. Soon I will not know the difference and being happy and energetic will be as normal to me as breathing is to me.

I will live my life as a happy and energetic person.

The 8th Sales Commandment

I will multiply myself and increase my value.

At one point or another everyone has wished they could duplicate or clone themselves. We've wished that so that we can work and sleep at the same time. So we could earn more money or sell to more people in the same time period. I've wished that I could multiply myself so I could duplicate my results dramatically and increase my value. I've never wished to multiply myself for the good things like, have an extra me around on vacation. Or have two of me sleeping in my bed at the same time. Every time I've ever wanted to multiply myself has always been to increase production, more sales so I could increase my value and now I will be able to multiply myself and increase my value. The greatest sales people in the world and successful people in general have learned the secret of multiplicity that has increased their values. They've learned how to multiply themselves which multiplies their results which in turn gives them more production, sales, money and even more time having fun with family and friends so I will multiply myself and increase my value.

I will multiply myself and increase my value.

Today I will work harder and smarter, not one or the other but both are necessary to multiply myself and increase my value. I will come up with and implement new ideas that will increase my production. I will master my products, tools and presentations so that my conversion ratios increase dramatically.

I will multiply myself and increase my value.

By mastering my products, tools and presentations I will be able to multiply myself. I will speak of my products and services so well that everyone I have spoken with will be able to duplicate what I have said to them with their family and friends. They will remember my powerful presentation and come back to meet with me again for added products and services and they will bring their family and friends. My associates will know I am the master of our products, tools and services and will also refer others to me knowing I am a master at what we do and wanting to provide the best for everyone whom they send my way which they will be rewarded with the knowledge of knowing they were still able to help everyone they have sent to me. I will reap the rewards of multiplicity that will also come when I've increased my value, and my income will begin multiplying itself. The quarters will turn to dollars and the dollars will turn to five dollars and the five to ten, and ten to one hundred and I will reap the rewards of my increased value.

I will multiply myself and increase my value.

I have read the 10 Sales Commandments and will continue to read each and everyday until I achieve everything I have set out to achieve. Sales can be the highest paid hard work or the lowest paid easy work. This is the profession I have chosen to be in and I can and will achieve all of my goals. I will reach all of my dreams.

I will follow the 10 sales commandments until I have reaped the rewards from the fruits of my labor that await me.

I choose to be a success and choose not to be a failure. The only way I fail is if I give up and that is something I will not do.

I do this not to prove anything to anyone else but myself. I choose to be a huge success and have more than I imagined possible not because of others but for myself. I do this to prove it to myself that first I can accomplish my mission and second for all of the rewards I will receive when I have accomplished what I have set out to accomplish.

I will do what ever it takes to succeed. The only failure there is, is giving up and I know I will not give up so I will succeed.

Chapter 1

The Sales Industry

The sales industry along with salespeople are what makes the world go around. The entire world is able to operate only because of the sales industry and salespeople. Just look around you. There isn't anything around you that didn't directly deal with the sales industry and a salesperson. If you're at home, look around you. Your television, it was sold to you by a salesperson. Your entertainment center the same thing. Your home, was sold to you by a salesperson and the mortgage for your home was given to you by another salesperson. What about your auto, dishes, pictures, etc, etc.

I know some of you have heard many times, things like. Well, I bought my dishes off of the shelf and not a salesperson, or my knives and what not. But even in situations that there isn't a salesperson directly involved in the sales process, there really was. How about the salesperson who sold the goods to the store? The salesperson that negotiated the deal to bring the products into the country? The salesperson that negotiated the manufacturing, delivery, quantity, price and the list goes on and on. As I said, the world as we know it revolves around the sales industry and salespeople!

Don't ever forget that.

Salespeople are the most successful professionals in the world! This is a fact! Salespeople are the highest paid professionals in any industry. Salespeople are also the most recognized but not always the way they should be. Salespeople in general are not given the proper respect they deserve and have earned. Salespeople are not given the same respect attorneys, doctors, accountants, and the like are given. Although we are more involved and do more for most consumers on a day to day basis, most salespeople are not given the respect they deserve.

This is not always the case. Generally speaking salespeople aren't looked at in the proper light. Good salespeople know this and don't dwell on it. A good salesperson is always positive with people who speak negative about their profession. A good salesperson is always speaking positively about their organization and industry and what they do. A good salesperson always represents themselves as a salesperson first and what exactly they sell second. This is something that should be done in the same sentence. I've always thought it to be sad when a salesperson describes themselves as something other than a salesperson. It's sad and most likely these salespeople will have many years of struggle ahead of them! Selling is a mindset. It's who we are. You can always tell the difference between a great salesperson and a mediocre salesperson. This also goes true for a veteran salesperson and a new one. Right from the beginning you could see the motivated, enthusiastic, new salesperson who will make it and the one that will not. You can tell right from the beginning who will make it or not. But don't let that fool you. Selling is also about persistency and consistency.

Everyone can succeed in the sales industry. That's right, it doesn't matter if you have talent, are energetic, enthusiastic, or any other quality that is not consistent with the top salespeople. If someone doesn't give up and they continue trying and improving their skills, they can and will succeed!

Believe it! I've trained many salespeople that did not have previous sales experience and all salespeople that have ever been under me have always been successful whole with me. I've had many

Like any industry there are good and bad sales companies and also good and bad salespeople. It will be up to us individually, as companies and leaders to change the way people view the sales industry and salespeople.

A great salesman once said "Sales is the highest paid hard work, or the lowest paid easy work".

We are all salespeople

Everyone is a sales person. We are all sales people. We all became sales people when we where very young. We became sales people with out even knowing it. Our parents and families knew. Although they may have not known it, they were training each of us to become sales people. They dressed us certain ways when we were children. We have been told how to act, speak, look.

They did this because they knew that we are all judged and in order to fit in and get what we want, we need to sell ourselves. In order to succeed and have more opportunity in life we must become sales people. I know our family and friends have not classified us as sales people, but we are and we learned from them at an early age. We have been trained to be sales people and as I said we are all sales people.

It is a shame that once we've mastered our sales skills at a very young age, our mothers and fathers realize that they are now scared to take us to the toy store because they know they will not be able to resist our persuasion skills. At a very young age, most children are at their peak sales ability.

So remember, there are sales people all around you all day, every day. Your accountant, doctor, lawyer, banker they are all sales people. When a doctor tells you what kind of medicine to buy and when to take it. He did not tell you this, he sold it to you. But like good and bad sales people a good doctor like a good sales person will get you to take it exactly as he sold it to you. Why, because exactly that, he sold it to you. The doctor that has less sales ability is the one that you will probably not listen to. When an attorney tells you how to proceed, he or she did not just tell you this, they sold it to you. When your accountant tells you how you must file your taxes, they sold the idea to you.

We believe them because we are not the experts, even with simple things such as children's bicycles. We trust the store associate who does not in most cases get paid any type of commission, but never the less is a salesperson. We rely on their expertise on which bicycle to buy. Which helmet to consider and in most cases we will buy the one they have recommended.

Remember, we do not have to take the medication the doctor recommended. We do not have to use the approach our attorney mentioned. We have the choice to say yes or no! We have the power to buy which ever bicycle we would like for our children. We are persuaded by sales people all day long. Even those sales people that do not get any type of commissions and do not care what we do sell us.

It is human nature to be a salesperson. Test it out. Ask someone of their opinion? I'd be willing to bet that they are going to try and persuade you to believe their opinion is right. It does not really matter what that opinion may even be. Just ask someone what they might think of a particular type of sink? Or automobile? Or even a particular color, and see what they will do. They will try to sell you what they are thinking or believe. Some might not be very good at it, while others are better and more aggressive.

Some will be more or less confident than others. Those are the same exact qualities all sales people have. The good ones, bad ones, wealthy ones, educated and not.

There are many types of sales people. You can classify them your selves or take what others have classified them as. There are good and bad sales people. There are experienced and non experienced sales people. The educated and uneducated sales people. So it would be very unwise to attempt to classify a sales person or sales people in general because of the type of work they do which is sales.

Chapter 2

The Sales people

There are many different types of sales people. Just like any industry there are good and bad sales people. There are the educated and non educated, intelligent and not. There are the flamboyant types. The fun and not so fun, etc. etc.

Sales people come from all walks of life. Some had silver spoons in their mouths, while others were very poor. Some sales people are trust fund babies while others earned every cent they ever had.

It would be unwise for anyone to try and attempt to classify sales people in any particular category, especially since as I have mentioned that they come form all walks of life and are very diverse. It would be like trying to classify doctors, attorneys, accountants, teachers or any other type of person based on what they do.

I am a true sales person and have been a sales person my entire life. I began selling at a very, very young age. Believe it or not, I was selling Avon door to door at the age of 8. As a young adult, I started a few different companies all of which were based on sales. Over the years I have personally recruited and trained several thousand sales people. I have studied sales people and have developed many other sales people that I knew had potential.

I am considered by many including myself to be an expert when it comes to sales and sales people.

I have traveled the country looking for and recruiting sales people. Over the years I have personally recruited and trained several thousand sales people.

In this chapter we will describe and categorize several types of sales people. We will cover the types of characteristics that make up the different types of sales people. To be honest, we will actually mention some of the categories, but really only focus on the great ones.

This is a motivational book and I'd like to make sure we focus on the positive so please understand, that although there are many types of salespeople our primary focus will be on the great ones.

Let us start by covering the first two categories that I am almost willing to bet each and every person has already placed sales people into. The good sales people and the bad sales people.

Now one must be very careful when discussing this very important topic. So when discussing the so called good and bad sales people, be very careful with your emotions. I have seen consumers classify a sales person as a bad one simple because they fell behind on their payments on what ever it is they have bought. In my eyes, that would not be the category I would place that sales person in that situation.

If someone over extended themselves by purchasing items they should not have or could not afford, that is not the sales persons responsibility. A sales person is not responsible for the spending habits of his or her clients. Furthermore, most sales people are optimistic. They would tend to think that their clients would earn more income and money as time passes. As they get promoted by their employers and earn more and more income, they should and could earn enough to buy anything they choose to have.

Most if not all sales people are optimistic and live by the same beliefs. Most sales people purchase items that they cannot always afford in the hopes and expectations that their income will increase.

Most sales people are driven!

The sales people that are not driven, if they stay in the sales business will become driven. It is inevitable not to become a driven sales person if they stay in sales. If they did, they would starve out of the business. Believe me when I tell you that most sales people are motivated and driven. The ones that have high expectations will purchase things they cannot afford at the time of purchase.

So as I mentioned before, one must be careful when they categorize a sales person.

On the flip side, I have seen and heard many consumers who considered a sales person to be a good one because they sold them a cheaper product. In their mind they know the sales person could have sold them the more expensive product, especially since they did not know about the cheaper product and were ready to purchase the more expensive product.

The consumer in this case did not realize that the cheaper product in this case does not have the quality of the more expensive product. The consumer in this case does not realize that the cheaper less quality product in reality is more expensive than the original higher priced product. They will spend additional money on repairs and additional stress and energy dealing with the situation, not to mention the fact that they will end up purchasing a new product to replace the one that is not in working order.

The consumer in this case that placed the salesperson that sold them this product on a pedestal by thinking that sales person was a good sales person. In many cases the consumer would not ever realize that the more expensive product would have still been in proper working condition and would last for several more years.

If the sales person in this case did not know of the actual quality of both products one might think that he could still be classified as a good sales person with the reasoning that they did not know about the better more expensive product.

Well, in my opinion this sales person should not be classified as a good sales person. If they were, they would have made it their responsibility to know which product in reality is better for their clients. If they were not sure or if they did not know about a newer product, then they should not be selling or recommending it to their clients.

In this example, I would not classify this sales person as a good one. That doesn't necessarily mean that they might not turn into one in the future, but at that moment they were negligent in their responsibilities to their client and also their company.

I would never sacrifice or promote a product that is not of the highest quality and best interest of my clients. A good and great sales person never does and never will. That does not necessarily mean I would not sell that product to my clients. Some of my clients at the time might not be able to afford the more expensive product at that time.

If that were the case, I absolutely would sell the less expensive product to my client. I would also make sure to explain the fact that it is of less quality and I would also comparer the two products. I would not down sell the less quality product, but I would make it clear that it is of less quality and what they should expect.

A good sales person would not ever sell something that is not of the highest quality, but in situations that their products are not the best or are of less quality as their competitors produscts. They will explain it to their clients because it still might be in their client's best interest.

Most products have a place in the market. Good and bad products alike have a place in the market. A good product is only good because of the sales person just as a bad product is only bad because of the sales person.

If a client buys the best product they can afford at the best price possible, if a good sales person explained the product properly and what their client should expect about the product. Then in that case the product is a good product!

We will be covering products in a later chapter.

For instance, a sales person that sells Honda automobiles is not doing his or her clients an injustice by selling them the Honda since a Mercedes Benz might be of higher quality.

In that case, I would have been looking out for the best interest of my client and my company. That is a win-win situation and is what good consumers and good sales people expect!

Does this make sense?

As you can plainly see, one must be careful when they categorize sales people as good or bad.

A simple rule of thumb I have for myself as a great sales person and my clients and company is this. It must be a win-win situation for all involved. If it is not, then they should not do business with me or I should not do business with them. It is as simple as that!

The extraordinary sales person

A great sales person is not merely a sales person. This is an amazing person. He or she does not just sell what they sell. They don't just sell their products or themselves. They can sell anything to anyone. They practice and work on honing their skills every moment of the day. You have seen them, the great sales people in any industry are very similar and act the same way.

They refuse to loose!

They negotiate their homes and get what they want, how they want it. They negotiate their automobiles and get what they want, how they want it. They negotiate everything and expect to get what they want. As I said before, they constantly hone and use their skills. They negotiate their hotels, auto rentals, dinners, clothing everything. They do this because they are great sales people and they know they can get what they want by using some of their tools. Keep in mind that these amazing sales people do this for a living. They are constantly negotiating with their clients and it is their job to persuade people to do what they want.

Like sales, it is a numbers game so they will not always get what they want, but they will most of the time. It becomes a game. Their confidence levels are so high, they know they cannot loose.

An incredible sales person has had years of successful experience. An incredible sales person can sell anything to anyone.

This breed of sales people are amazing and can literally walk into any office and sell anything. They do not need to be an expert at their products or their industry and will have success.

There is no other industry like sales. If you are an even good sales person you can make it in any industry, but you would make it by selling. In other words you continue doing what you do best, which is sell. No other profession offers this type of guaranteed success to those that are great at what they do.

For instance, Michael Jordan is considered by most to be the best basketball player to have ever played the game. I think everyone would agree that he has amazing talent and has amazing skills. Not only that, but he's gifted. He has natural ability. So although he is gifted, dedicated, intelligent, etc, etc. That alone does not guarantee that he can use those skills that he is best at in other industries or sports. For instance, Michael Jordan tried it. He went on to play another sport. Remember, he played baseball for awhile. He tried his best. He used his talent, motivation and abilities and never really amounted to much as a baseball player. It wasn't because of lack of persistence or lack of effort. It was simple because being an expert in one sport and having all the ability in the world does not mean you can apply those same skills in other industries or sports.

This does not even mean Michael Jordan was not good. He looked pretty good to me, but being pretty good does not cut it. Many, many individuals are good. But being merely good is not being great or the best at something.

Let us look at other professional athletes. Like a great athlete, a great actor let us say Micky Roark for instance. He is a great actor and one of the best. He also tried to be great at something else. He went on to box. I have seen a couple of his matches and I liked his style and thought he was good. I was also amazed at how he was able to transform his physique into a boxers physique. He looked like a professional body builder. He looked and was strong. He also had some good skills. He did not take this lightly just like Michael Jordan did not.

So he became a professional boxer. He was pretty good. But as I have said before, just being pretty good at something does not mean you will be great at it. Although you might be the best at something in a particular industry, you will most likely not be able to transform that greatness into another industry as you could with sales.

With sales, if you are a great sales person, you could be great at selling automobiles and have huge success. If you are one of the best sales persons at any firm, you will most likely be one of the best sales persons in any sales office. So if you switched industries and went from selling automobiles you could then go into the mortgage business and be one of the top producers selling mortgages. You could go into financial services and be one of the top producers there as well.

You could sell anything in any industry. If you decided to sell art work, you would be a top producer there as well. As I said before, there is not another industry that you could be one of the best in that you can use those same skills in other industries.

For those of you that are thinking, well those industries are different; they could not go into the medical industry. These special breed of incredible sales people could go into the medical field and sell medical supplies.

Get it? A great sales person can sell anything to anyone. You must keep in mind that most great sales people like to live life well, so just because they could sell anything to anyone they are not going to make foolish decisions and switch from selling a high ticket item, such as mortgages, real estate, and mortgages to lower ticket items such as automobiles. Do not get me wrong. I know plenty of auto sales people that earn over $100,000 per year. I have even met one auto sales person who earns over $300,000 per year.

I could also be the best auto sales person in any lot, but I would have to work a lot harder and put in a lot more hours to earn the income I earn now. So I would not misuse my talents switching industries where I would have to work twice as much and twice as hard to earn the same amount of income. That wouldn't be a smart thing to do, nor would I recommend that to anyone.

I am not trying to insult any industry; it is also a matter personality. Some might have more success selling autos because they like it more. My example is only referring to the fact that a great sales person can sell anything in any industry and have success.

Most great sales people are not known. Some are but most people would not consider them sales people.

Donald Trump for instance is an amazing and great sales person. Most would not consider him a sales person, but that is exactly what he is. He is a deal maker. He is not merely a business man; he is much more than that. He is an amazing sales person. As I have said before, a great sales person can duplicate his results in any industry, and as you well know, Donald Trump is in many different industries and he makes things happen because that is who he is and he can. He is a great sales person so what ever he wants he gets.

The list of great sales people goes on and on.

Bill Gates, yes he knows computers. Yes he might be brilliant, but do not let the fact that he knows computers fool you. He is an amazing sales person. Yes, he is a sales person and like most great sales people he is an opportunist. I use that term in a very positive sense. As I said before, most sales people including myself are opportunists.

In my opinion Bill Gates biggest success was not inventing or creating Windows operating system, because he did not. Steve Job created Windows. So in my opinion, and as I have said, Bill Gates is an opportunist and an amazing sales person, so when Bill Gates saw Windows he knew he could sell it to the world. Since he is a sales person and he knows his ability as an amazing sales person. He knew he could get what he wanted. He knew that he could sell Windows and become a billionaire, but he knew he could also negotiate and buy the rights to Windows and then own the rights and then sell it to the world. Knowing what you know, you already know Bill Gates owns Windows and has already sold it to the world.

There are a million stories just like those, but one of my favorites is the story of the Colonel! You know who I am referring to. I am referring to KFC, the Colonel. He is one of the greatest sales people I have ever learned about. Most would also consider him to be a restaurant owner or being in the food industry when he was much more than that. He was an amazing sales person.

For those of you that do not know the story, you should go out and learn about it. But I will indulge you and tell you a little bit about it now. The Colonel didn't start out owning restaurants or even making chicken. He did love chicken and had his own recipe to make chicken taste great! That is all he had, it was a recipe. But to an amazing sales person who would sell anything to anyone, this is an opportunity. To an amazing great sales person this is an opportunity of a lifetime.

So the Colonel knew he had something of value. So with no money, and a recipe, he went out and started visiting restaurants. Back then there was no fast food or chicken restaurants, back then the most popular restaurants were burger joints. So he went out and talked the burger joints into selling his fried chicken with his special recipe.

He guaranteed his results and persuaded the restaurant owners to try it and to watch their sales soar.

It sure worked. His recipe and way of cooking chicken was such a huge success and people loved it and could not get enough of it so much that most burger joints started selling only the fried chicken.

The Colonel was such an amazing and incredible sales person that he never sold the most important part which was his secret recipe. So he had all the control. He manufactured his own recipe and if the restaurants didn't cook the chicken the exact way he had instructed he would cancel their order and not sell them the special sauce.

The restaurant owners had experienced the success his recipe has brought them and would not attempt not to obey his instructions.

After selling to restaurant owners for a few years, he had created an established clientele of over five hundred (500) restaurants that he provided the special sauce for their chicken.

This is amazing, keep in mind that he did not own any of these restaurants at the time, but created success for himself and the restaurants. Not because he was a great restaurant owner, but because he was a great sales person.

Now that was one of my favorite stories, but let me share with you my favorite. My favorite and in my opinion one of the best sales people in the world is Ray Kroc! For those of you that don't recognize the name he was the founder of McDonalds.

For those of you that are not familiar with the story, I would highly recommend reading about it, it could change the way you sell and make you an amazing sales person. Ray Kroc also was not a restaurant owner nor was he in the food business. He was an amazing super sales person!! That is a fact.

Ray Kroc started out selling milk shale makers to restaurants. His best seller was what he called the multi mixer. It was a milk shale maker that could make several milk shakes at once. At that time there were no fast food joints, however burger and milk shake joints were very popular. So Ray Kroc was very successful selling his multi mixers. He had heard of this restaurant far away that had a higher level of success than any of the restaurants he had ever worked with so he decided to make a trip and visit this restaurant. When he got there, he was amazed at how many people this restaurant could serve.

They were making primarily burgers and shakes so they were able serve quite a bit more people than other restaurants that had to cook many other meals.

Ray Kroc thought this would be a great way to sell his multi mixers! The restaurant was owned and operated by the McDonald brothers and was called McDonalds.

The brothers were amazed by Ray Kroc and loved the multi mixer. Ray Kroc wanted to sell more multi mixers and being the opportunistic super sales person he was, he convinced the McDonald brothers to open more and more McDonalds restaurants. He knew this would earn them all a large amount of money, and he knew this was a great way to sell his multi mixers. That was his original motivation. He just wanted to sell more of his multi mixers.

The rest as you know is history. Well there is a lot more than that, so I would encourage all to pick up his story and read about him. He truly is an amazing super sales person.

As I said before, most people do not know of these super amazing sales people. Or do not consider these business people to be sales people, when in reality that is exactly what they are!

Let me give you an example of a sales person you might recognize. It is from a fictional character out of a movie. The movie is Beverly Hills Cop Axel Foley, was the cop that in reality is an amazing sales person. He could persuade anyone to do what ever he wanted. Now I would not recommend people to use his tactics, his tactics involved many different antics, but remember this is a movie.
I loved this character and he is a super sales person in the movie, but remember he was not considered a sales person.

If you would like to become a great sales person I would encourage you to rent this movie and adapt his enthusiasm, motivation and attitude. If you have always wanted to see how an incredible sales person acts, rent this movie and look at how he acts. He does not get down when adversity presents itself. He is not surprised when things go wrong. He does not give up when he is on a mission. He does not care about the consequences or struggles he must go through to achieve his goal.

He was always selling himself which is one of the most important things a sales person must do.

Once again, I am not saying I liked his tactics. My point is only he has the hear of a super sales person and I personally have used some of his energy and motivation in my sales skills and it has worked for me and I know can work for you.

That being said, yes I know he miss led people and has lied in the movie, that is one of the things I love. Not the lies or miss leading, but it motivates me to know that he had to lie. A great sales person does not have to. I don't have to either. If he can sell his point of view with lies to people. If he had to miss lead people in order to convince them to do something he wanted, then great sales people could sell the truth! If he could sell some outrageous story to someone and get people to believe these outrageous tales, and he did.

I loved the fact that I should be able to sell things that make sense! So could you! You could sell the truth because the truth makes sense. People understand and believe the truth, especially since it makes sense!

Not only that, but they can see the sincerity when you explain it. It looks and feels a lot different to you the sales person and the consumer who hears it from you. Believe me when I tell you that they can feel it, so can you.

So take what you can from these extraordinary sales people and learn from them. They have some great stories because they were great people. The stories did not just happen to them, they created them. You could do the same.

These are just a few stories of many thousands just like them. You should make it a goal to go out and discover some of these stories and others like them for yourself. I guarantee they could change your life. I know learning about these stories sure did for me.

The Mind of a great sales person

Great sales people are highly motivated and are very optimistic people. In order to be successful and great sales people they must be. The sales industry is already filled with such negative feelings and situations that a great sales person understands they do not want to add more to it.

Keep in mind that all great sales people have spent many years honing and mastering their techniques, so everything they do is for a reason. Being motivated and optimistic is also something they do on purpose, and not by accident.

Great sales people have many similar characteristics, for instance. Most if not all sales people I have met with read motivational books. Books on business, sales, marketing, and self help books. There are many reasons they read these types of books. One of the main reasons is because sales is not taught in schools. Sales is not taught in elementary, high school or college. Sales itself is not considered an industry.

For that reason anyone that would like to be great in sales will in fact have to read these types of books. If they do not, it will be a hard tough road of trial and error.

Although there are many great companies that provide sales training in their industry, the great sales people have already realized that is not enough.

If you go into any successful organization, you could compare the sales person with the best results or most sales to the sales person with the lowest or worse sales and realize you may not know why.

It would be obvious to compare them together and you would see some things that are common. Their attitudes, attire, etc, etc. I'm not referring to those qualities. I'm referring to the sales people that are alike. Compare two motivated sales people who dress similar, who come from similar backgrounds. If you compared those sales people you would most likely not be able to give me a reason as to why they get different results.

Compare two sales people that work for the same company and have received the same sales material, who have also received the same sales training, who sell the same product at the same prices. You would most likely not be able to tell me why one would outsell the other.

This is because of many factors involved. If one of the sales people wanted to be better or get better results than another, how could he or she achieve this? If they had the same training, sell the same thing, then how could one possible get better results than the other?

The answer is, one would do additional research and get some books. One would go to seminars. As he or she learns more about sales, they would also learn about more and more resources they did not know of.

Being a great sales person is much more than just dressing well. It is much more than just speaking well, or being flamboyant or having people like you. Being a great sales person requires much more than that. You could be the best dressed, most flamboyant sales person in the world, but with out new fresh leads or prospects, how would you get sales?

So as a sales person who strives to become great learns more about sales, they will eventually discover that knowing how to sell is not the only important thing. Because eventually they will have read enough and been to enough sales seminars to learn how to speak, act, and dress, they will some day be a well dressed well spoken sales person with no prospects to speak with.

That realization in itself will then motivate them to research marketing. This well trained sales person would now be interested in learning about direct mail, networking, elevator speech, referrals, etc, etc. As a sales person each one of these categories also requires sales ability. Each category requires

When they have discovered marketing then marketing will

The Body of a great sales person

As I have mentioned before. Great sales people are over achievers. They are winners and refuse to loose. This is not only the criteria that they live by in their business and sales lives, this is who they are as people. That being said, it should be obvious that a great sales person would also not want to loose in the looks department. A great sales person would like to look their best at all times. Part of looking their best is not only in the clothing and grooming. A large part of how they look in their clothes is their body.

Do not be fooled by thinking a great sales person is not an athlete. A great sales person focus and work as hard on their bodies as they do with their sales and business careers. In order to maintain their level of energy and performance they must. They know their bodies are also their greatest asset.

Their bodies are very finely toned machines. They work on their speech, posture, body language and appearance. All of these things are directly connected with their body. Their language, posture and physiology would not look and be the same without having their bodies in top condition.

Great sales people must maintain their physiques, not only for the appearance factor, but also because they deal with a great amount of pressure. Pressure stemming from a lot of different circumstances that the average professional athlete does not have to deal with.

The pressures and stress great sales people face

A day in the life of a great sales person would consist of a lot of stress. Stress such as rejection, and a lot of it. They will get rejected more in one day than the average person will go through in an entire month.

They will also have to face management pressures. Although great sales people are self starters, the fact that they are top producers in it self tends to create a lot of additional pressure and stress from management. Since they are a top producer and a great sales person, their management immediately expect more from them.

Not only do they expect more, but they are the go to person when things are not exactly where they should be. When the company has not hit their goals or quotas, they start at the top of the food chain and go directly to the top producers first.

Great sales people also have the ability to motivate others around them. Enthusiasm is contagious, so when they are motivated, they tend to motivate others around them.

The changes in the economy whether for the better or worse also contributes to the pressure and stress levels great sales people.

If the economy gets worse, then consumers in general tend to slow their spending in all industries. So then the great sales people do not just sit there and try and wait it out. As I have said before and will continue to say, they refuse to loose and is one of the qualities that make a great sales person. So in trying times the great sales people will figure out a way to over come the economy and market. They will work harder, smarter come up with better ways to attract new business. They will find a way to win. It is in their blood, it is who they are.

Some would think that during good economies the great ones would not have pressure and stress. That is not the case. During good economies when consumers tend to spend more money in a lot of industries, the great sales people try and cope with the surge in business. They refuse to loose and will need to figure out how to handle double or even triple their normal volume of new business which in itself creates added pressure.

Some other pressure and stress great sales people will encounter is customer attitudes, customer issues and problems, budgets, long hours, time management, family, friends, etc. Great sales people want to please everyone and want to be the best always.

It is sad to know that most sales people that go through similar pressure and stresses do not take positive action in dealing with the pressure and stress that come along with the sales industry.

Most sales people deal with these issues reactively than proactively and do not take the extra steps necessary needed to handle these situations better. They tend to neglect their bodies. Of course these would not be the great sales people.

A great sales person is pro active and do not wait until something happens in order for them to react. They are proactive and react before something happens and in most cases change the course of the matter at hand, therefore not having to react at all. They anticipate these things and help lower their pressure and stress levels.

Great sales people know they must maintain their bodies in order to be in peek performing condition to be efficient and be able to handle all of these situations along with the ones they expect, but are yet unaware of.

Eating Habits of great sales people

Maintaining their bodies and physiques is not as easy as just exercising. It takes a healthy diet and will power.

I have always studied people and one of the largest groups of individuals I have ever studied are sales people. I have seen many, many sales people with very poor eating habits. I have seen them go to fast food joints and splurge. These are obviously not the top producing sales people. Sales people that do not care about their appearance or keeping their bodies in peak condition at that moment are not typically the great sales people.

Don't get me wrong, I have also seen top producing great sales people that frequent these establishments. The great sales people still maintain some will power and will eat light meals. They will also tend to eat a lot of salads.

Some of the great sales people do not have the time to sit down at restaurants and wait for a meal. They also tend to meet their clients in their homes, place of business etc. They are usually on the run.

That is not always the case.

I have seen many great sales people that are at a whole new level that never leave their office and always meet their clients and prospects in their office. These great sales people also eat at a sit down restaurant every day for lunch and spend at least 1-2 hours at lunch. They also rarely if ever miss a lunch.

Take a look at some of the great sales people in the country and great leaders. These top producers have a large amount of pressure and stress on a daily basis. These top producers will face more pressure and stress in a month than the average person will fac in a lifetime. Their ability to be able to not only handle pressure and stress but to achieve during these challenging times also makes them who they are as top producers.

If you have ever studied these top producers, you will notice that they maintain their bodies with exercise.

You have seen presidents and billionaires who not only exercise on a regular basis but also eat healthy light meals.

Many find that exercising helps reduce their stress levels along with helping them create new levels of energy which will help them maintain or even increase their production and productivity. Many great sales people exercise in the mornings before work. They feel it helps with their creativity and helps them get prepared for their day.

Exercise provides many great things, not just in appearance and health, but also with your emotions. Exercising releases and produces endorphins which is the feel good drug in your brain

Before starting an exercise program, you should first check with your physician.

If you are motivated and ready to start an exercise program, just remember that like anything worth while will take effort and commitment and will not come easy.

Don't get discouraged. If you have not exercised in a while it might take a little longer to start getting the rewards you deserve and want.

Stick with it and I can assure you that your efforts will be rewarded ten times fold!!

Sleeping habits of great sales people

By now you are starting to get a pretty good picture of great sales people. You are starting to understand that great sales people are a breed all their own. Although anyone with some determination can also become a great sales person, most are not willing to put the effort required to do so.

Great sales people are very passionate people and live life to its fullest. They tend to push life to its limit and is one of the driving forces that help them be a great sales person.

Everyone needs sleep. Great sales people need it more than others. Great sales people work hard and play even harder. They push their business life to the limit along with their personal lives.

They work hard and long hours. They will work until the job is done and the sale is closed.

They will also make the best of their personal time. They will travel, entertain, boat, camp, jog, etc, etc. They will go out to nice dinners, theatre, shows, comedy clubs and such. They use their time very wisely as with their business they will maximize their time. Keep in mind that is one of the motivating factors why they work hard, so they can play harder. They consider this type of living also a recharge of their bodies and mind.

The life of great sales people takes a lot of energy. Since they use their energy, they must replenish it with sleep. They are not couch potatoes and will not waste away precious time relaxing on the couch or in bed. They will need to replenish their energy with sleep.

They need sleep for much more than just energy. They need the physical rest as well.

In order for great sales people to be at their peak, they need and must get rest. This is something they will need to have will power with. Great sales people live great lives and must make the time for rest. It is easy to get caught up in the life and put off something as important as sleep, but that would be a big mistake.

If you want to become a great sales person you must get sleep. You should go to bed early and wake up early, refreshed and ready to face the day.

It will take discipline and sheer will to make yourself get to bed at a reasonable hour in order for you to be focused, prepared, ready and rested for the day.

If you are serious about becoming a great sales person you should be in peak physical and mental condition and one way of doing it is getting sleep.

Great sales people are great problem solvers

It should start becoming very clear why great sales people are great. They are great at many skills. Being a great sales person is much more than just being able to talk with people and getting people to like you.

Many people have the misconception that all it takes is a golden tongue to be a great sales person. Well, for those of you that believe that and continue believing that, it would be plain to see why you would continue being merely a sales person instead of a great sales person.

If you want to be a great sales person, follow these rules of the great sales people and you to can be a great sales person. But it takes all of these things and then some, to be one of the great ones!

I am glad it takes this type of effort to be a great sales person. I am elated to know that it takes hard work and it takes being great at a lot of different things to be a great sales person. If it didn't, then all of us would be great instead of just a few. I know I will always be one of the great ones, because I am willing to put in this kind of relentless effort. I also know that most are not willing to put this type of effort, so I am guaranteed a good standing in the sales industry.

For those of you that are not willing to be merely a sales person, thank you. You motivate me to continue giving my best effort and you keep me keeping on.

Great sales people are great problem solvers. They are constantly problem solving. That is one of the main criteria to be a great sales person. How could they not be great problem solvers. They have problem solved for their clients and helped them solve their problems with their products and services.

That's what they do, is problem solve.

When they face rejection they have to immediately come up with another solution to the over come the problem. When yet another objection or rejection comes along, they have to come up with yet another solution to the problem.

They not only problem solve, they are experts at problem solving. They do this in the most difficult of situations. They do this in situations when the person they are problem solving for is typically in a negative state of mind. They do this in situations when the other person is not being to attentive. And they do it well!

They not only problem solve in tough situations, but they do it with a smile on their face and do it while still winning over their clients. They are able to problem solve in the right situations and also be able to present it in such a way that it makes sense to their prospect or client.

Keep in mind that when they are presenting their skills as a great problem solver they are doing it in situations that their clients have the upper hand. The client does not want to look as if they are giving in. The client did not want to think that they couldn't come up with that solution. So the great sales person must use some of their other talents when problem solving as well.

Great problem solvers are not merely problem solvers, they are also great presenters as well. It is one thing to come up with a great solution to a problem, but if it is not presented well, then your solution may not ever get put into action.

So when problem solving, or overcoming objections which in my mind are one of the same make sure that you also remember that you must communicate and present this in such a way as to persuade or sell your solution to the prospect or client.

Great problem solvers were not born that way, they were created by years and years of problem solving. They have become experts by problem solving. Problem solving does not also mean that you will come up with the right solution the first time. It may take several attempts or solutions to finally accomplish the end result. Isn't that what problem solving is all about?

Great problem solvers are also confident. They are not always so sure that the problem will get solved the first time. They are sure and confident that they arte making a decision and something is going to happen.

Sir Isaac Newton once said "To every action there is an equal and opposite reaction". Great problem solvers understand this principle very well and is why they make decisions, knowing that their decision will create another reaction and if they continue making enough decisions they will end up with the end result which is where they want to go.

Think about it?

Let me give you a great example. An airplane is off course over ninety percent (90%) of the time, yet they make it to their final destination. How do they do that? Well the answer is quite simple. They keep maneuvering the plane towards the final destination, over and over and over again. The pilot was essentially wrong in their problem solving skills ninety percent (90%) of the time.

All the pilot had to do was keep changing the course over and over and over again to finally win, accomplish the mission, achieve or how ever you would like to label it. Well not only that. The pilot also had to continue and not give up in order to achieve the end result. So in order to be a great problem solver you must also be persistent and consistent. The bottom line is the pilots problem solving skills worked and they made it.

Being a great problem solver does not mean getting the right answer the first time. It may and most likely take many, many decisions to end with the right answer or solution to the problem.

So if you want to be a great problem solver, start making some decisions. Start not only making some decisions, but also think of the way you would present your solution. Practice. Roll play, do it over and over again. Think outside of the box. Think and voice several ideas and opinions.

When selling be very careful and you should only come up with solutions you have the answer to. If not you will encounter some resistance or rejections that you will not be prepared to handle at that exact moment.

I have a great problem solving story for you, I remember hearing a story of a trucker that had a very large load of some very expensive cargo to deliver somewhere. This truck was too high by just one inch and could not make it through a tunnel. This was a very big problem since the company needed the products in order to have their company survive and the state had a large interest in solving this problem also because it was becoming a problem with traffic and was putting peoples lives in danger. This was definitely becoming a problem. The product was much too large to unload and they would have the same problem with another truck the same size. It was too heavy to airlift.

After all this time, there were about 15-20 separate people trying to figure out what to do. The media was also there covering the story and it was becoming a big issue. Not to mention the tens of thousands of dollars spent trying to figure the solution out. A little girl came by and asked, why don't they just empty some of the tires.

Wow, now that is thinking out side of the box. Yes everyone was doing the right things and eventually they would have come up with an answer, but thinking out of the box, may speed the process up all the while by making you look like a genius.

Think about that story for a moment. How simple is the answer? And for those of you wondering, yes it worked. That's all it took.

Problem solving is a skill and one that could be developed and one that can be improved.

If you would like to become a great problem solver think out side of the box. Do brain teases, play chess, do cross word puzzles.

Learn new things, read how others have over come some problems and solved them.

If you don't understand something, learn about it so it makes more sense. Who knows, maybe knowing how the light bulb works might help you run your business better.

Challenge yourself. Listen to classical music. Classical music has been studied and shows that it stimulates the mind.

Also get others involved. Major corporations and teams have regular problem solving meetings and in reality most new and fresh ideas typically come from the people not directly involved and ones that are not the top executives.

The Discipline of a great sales person

It would be foolish for me or anyone to believe that selling and the sales industry is easy. It would be equally as foolish to think that it is a hard industry to be in, or that not anyone can succeed in the sales.

For what ever reason you have thought of or have already begun a wonderful career in sales, one thing is for sure.

It will be up to you and only you to decide what kind of sales person you will be. It will ultimately depend solely upon you, your determination, enthusiasm, motivation, persistence or the lack there of which will determine your level of success or failure.

The great sales people are all very disciplined individuals. Although I have seen many successful sales people that over the years have lost some of their disciplined qualities, you better believe that at one point that person indeed was very disciplined. You cannot achieve the level of a great sales person with out being disciplined.

I'm sure most of you would agree that if you followed these simple yet affective things, your success in sales would increase.

Some of your levels of success would increase dramatically maybe quadrupling or more your highest level of success while others may only double their prior successes.

I'm sure everyone could agree that applying some of these effective techniques would and could increase your sales, income and over all quality of life. That being said, I'm sure a lot of you are already thinking of reasons why you could not do these simple yet effective exercises. A lot of you are already trying to convince yourself why this would not work for you or your exact situation. You might be telling yourself that it is because you are a single parent, as am I and most people I know. Or you might be telling yourself that you are new in the sales industry and have not yet learned what you need in order to be successful, as are most people I work with. Maybe it is because you say you are too old, or maybe even too young. Maybe it is because your product is too expensive or not expensive enough, or the economy, or your company just does not provide you with enough quality leads.

I have heard it all, I just stopped with the most common things I hear constantly. There are many more that I refuse to acknowledge. The bottom line is, you need to make the decision how successful you want to be in sales. You need to make the commitment as to how much income you are going to make, how many prospects you will speak with, how many you will meet with, and then how many will you sell.

You need to be a fine toned disciplined athlete. That is what all great sales people are like.

Great sales people are very disciplined and follow certain scientific rituals that guarantees their success.

With out their discipline they could not succeed. With out their discipline they could never become a great sales person.

There is a myth about great sales people. The great sales people make it look easy. They always seem as if they are on clod nine, which they are most of the time. Remember they are great sales people.

Once they have reached this level of success, there is no reason why they should not be.

They have already put in their dues. Already went through the good and bad days, weeks, and even years. They have already mastered the art of selling. It has already been programmed in their inner being what it takes to reach and maintain the level of success they have chosen for themselves. They have reached their chosen level of success and not only have the ability to maintain, but they have the confidence to back it up. They know in their gut that they can, will and do succeed.

They have all of the toys, houses they want. They take numerous vacations several times per year. The great sales people have all the time they desire with their family and friends.

It is great to be a great sales person.

This is why and how the myth has begun. Many people have seen these great sales people with their boats, motorcycles, sports cars and their fancy homes and clothes that they have come up with their own ideas about it.

These great sales people have everything and are always happy, enthusiastic, motivated, energetic, etc, etc. They have become myths.

"The great sales people have everything and are always happy, enthusiastic, motivated, energetic"

Now there are many myths about the great sales people which has also flowed down into the sales industry as a whole in many cases.

As with any great athlete, professional, or great person in general. When you are great at something, you are going to make it look easy. Of course a great sales person has a smile on their face, they are happy as they should be. Why not?

Of course the great ones are happy, they just closed a sale, got a new prospect, had another great idea or just had a great sales rally.

Maybe they just opened their commissions check, bought a new car, or had a great lunch meeting.

They are experts at sales. This comes naturally for them, although it might not have always been the case. But we're talking about the great ones, so if they are great, you can bet your bottom dollar that it does now.

So since the great sales people are happy, have nice things, enjoy their life and their families and friends love them. Since they do this and love doing it, they make it look easy. Since they have more time on their hands spending with their family and friends, since they have the time and money available to take more vacations than the average person does, most people have begun putting a twist on it.

These facts have allowed several myths to come about. One of the biggest myth in sales is that it is easy. It sometimes surprises me how some people see a great sales person and say, well I can do that! I can spend all day on the golf course and take vacations and then just work 20 hours a week and be successful.

If I lived that life, I could be successful also. I would be successful since I would not have to stress out about my finances, or my family. I would always be recharged and would not always feel burned out. I could do that.

What a misconception and fallacy!

Little do they realize that this person is a specialist and an expect in his or her field of sales. Little do they realize that this person is one of the most disciplined people they have ever looked at which is why they have reached the levels of success that they have reached.

Little do they know the trials and errors these great sales people had to face, or the countless peanut butter and jelly sandwiches they had to eat.

These people do not realize how many countless nights were spent in the office, or how many nights while they were at home watching television with their family, the great sales people were in some office at midnight trying to make something happen. The nights they had to meet a client at their place of business one and a half hours away and the only time the client could meet with you was at 8pm in their home, which guarantees the great sales person would not be back in their home until after 10pm.

It never surprises me how people think they can just be great. It's funny to me how I never hear these same people with these misconceptions say, I know this doctor that is very successful that works only twenty hours per week and has a boat and toys and takes a lot of vacations. Man, I could do that. I could be a doctor like them. Or I could be a brain surgeon, or attorney.

Why is it we never hear these same people speaking of how they could be a scientist, brain surgeon and such. Well the answer is simple. They believe it took some hard work for the doctors, attorneys and such to become successful. They know it took a lot of time and effort and many, many, many years of school that they were not willing to put in to become a doctor, or attorney.

It is not that they did not think they could.

Many of them know they could, but also know they were not willing to put in the late nights of studying that the doctor put in.

They know they did not want to put in that type of effort. They did not want to have the overnight study groups.

Little do they know that the great sales people put in the same type of effort as a doctor, attorney and the like. Since there are no master degree programs for sales people, the average person is unaware of the type of discipline it takes to be a great sales person.

The myth that a doctor or attorney has more discipline than a great sales person is truly that, a myth. I have met many doctors and attorneys alike that did not have the discipline I have, or that other great sales people have. Yes, I know they went to school for many years. Yes I know they were poor before they became doctors and had to support themselves and ate top ramon. Yes I know that while others were having a good ole time they were studying. Yes I know the discipline they had to get to bed early, and to learn.

That is my point exactly, so did the great sales people!

Do not let the fact that there is no masters or doctorates degrees for the sales industry fool you. Great sales people are as disciplined as doctors and attorneys and it takes the same type of effort. They must be disciplined in order to achieve their level of success, just like any other profession, including doctors and attorneys.

Great sales people have put in their dues and have made sacrifices. Their families have also sacrificed with the long hours, late hours, stress, lack of money, studying, practicing, etc. After all of that the ones that stick with it will inevitable reap the rewards just like the ones who stuck it out in school to become doctors.

So if you are starting a career in sales or have many years under your belt already, know this. If you want to be a great sales person, you can. But do not be fooled for a minute that it might come easy. Or that it will not take strong discipline in order to achieve the level of success that you are looking for, because that is not the case.

I have always put in a great deal of effort and have been disciplined. I have always had great success in sales, but it still took me many years to realize the amount of discipline I had to have in order to reach the levels of success I wanted. Don't get me wrong, I have had fun. I have had the boats, motorcycles, vacations, the rovers, bmw's. I have lived the life of a rock star and have no complaints, but had I known the discipline I had to maintain, I would have still had the fun, but would have reached the level of success I wanted quicker and easier.

Great sales people must be disciplined not only with their work ethic, but also in with their;
- Attitude
- Attire
- Grooming
- Eating
- Sleeping
- Exercising
- Learning
- Practicing
- Prospecting
- Presenting
- Communication

These are just a few things that great sales people are great at and in order to become a great sales person these are the things that you will need to master and be disciplined with.

"Great sales people are very disciplined and follow certain scientific rituals that guarantees their success"

"A great sales person will get rejected more in one day than the average person will go through in an entire month"

Mimicking an extraordinary sales person

The best way to become an extraordinary sales person is to look at what they do. Look at how they do it. Watch how they act. Watch how they dress, etc. You should try to find someone you admire and respect that is where you would like to be. Start imaging them, do what they do. Act how they act. Dress how they dress. Work like they work, and soon, you will start achieving higher levels of success.

By imaging and doing what an extraordinary sales person would you, would bring you higher levels of success. The reason is quite simple. They have already discovered what it takes to achieve the levels of success that you are looking for.

Everyone can achieve! We are all born winners and can achieve. We just all have not learned what it will take to achieve our goals yet. It takes a lot of trial and error before we discover it.

Behind every extraordinary sales person is a person who as already tried and failed. They have done it so much, that they have learned from it and now do what works.

They have also put in their dues and know what it takes to succeed. They have already discovered how many hours it will take to reach their goals. They know how many people they must meet, how many presentations they must do, how many sales they must get. They have these numbers all figured out.

Go out and start doing what the successful extraordinary sales people do. If you know one of them, ask if you could work with them. Ask them if they could use any extra help. I'm sure most of them would let you.

Extraordinary sales people are great communicators and teachers. That is one of the things that help them become very successful. They are able to communicate very well with others and when others understand what they are trying to say, they buy.

Be a go getter! I have told this same thing to many new sales people. I am never surprised by how many wanna be sales people tell me they cannot work as hard as so and so. Or how many say, they are not willing to work that hard. Or how many have told me that they want to play, or they need more time with their families, or this that and the other.

It is sad, but in order to have all of these things they must work hard. It is almost impossible to become successful in any industry without putting any effort into it.

I do not care how much natural talent you have. Or how flamboyant you are, or how great of anything. It is all irrelevant and you must put in not only effort, but a lot of time also in order to become a successful sales person. Believe me, there is no easy way about it. Do not get me wrong, I am not saying that you will not be able to start a career in sales. I am simple saying that if you want to become an extraordinary sales person, you must put in a lot of effort, and time and there will be struggle.

All of your dreams can and will come true when you do!

If you fail to put in the necessary time and work. All of the things you want, you will have even less of. You want to play, well without the necessary funds you will play less when you work less.

You want more time with your family, you will eventually have to work more when you work less, because then you will need the extra time and money to spend with your family. It is not the other way around.

You want happiness, well you will not be able to have it if you do not put the necessary time and effort in, because you will be so stressed about finances, bills and your commissions that you will not be able to use the time you have on productive fulfilling things that would help you and your family.

The New Sales Person

It is sad to say that most sales people that start a career in sales have a miss conception. Most of them started a career in sales because they have known a sales person who made a lot of money. Or they have seen sales people for themselves and wanted to earn a lot of money.

Regardless of whether they know someone or read about someone or just simple think they can earn a lot of money, one thing is for sure. In sales everyone has the opportunity to have a successful career. Everyone that joins the sales force has the opportunity to earn a large income.

Sales people have the opportunity to earn as much as doctors, lawyers and even professional athletes. That is right, good and even decent sales people have the opportunity and do earn as much as doctors, lawyers, accountants, plastic surgeons and the list goes on and on.

Great sales people earn as much as professional athletes and actors. A great sales person will earn even more money than professional sports players along with actors and actresses.

A new sales person coming starting out in sales knows this and want a piece of the American dream. A new sales person entering the business of sales does not expect or think they will be one of the ones earning more than professional sports players or actors and actresses. No one can really predict that.

Some great sales people many times settle for a lot less than that, although they will most likely still be in the top 5% of the highest paid people in the country.

There are no limits on what a sales person can earn. There is no limitations as to what industry any new sales person can be in. Living the American dream can be achieved by being or becoming a new sales person.

Quality of life is another very strong driving force for new sales people. Money is most likely the highest driving force, but for many entering the sales industry, quality of life is also a strong motivating factor.

Think about it. A career where you can earn as little or as much as you like and work your own hours. A career where you can spend more time with your family and be able to drop your children off to school every day and even pick them up. A sales career where you can take extra time off and have the income to enjoy more quality time with your family.

Those are the two main reasons people join the sales industry. There is how ever another reason we touched on a little. That was the fact that some may not have the education needed to earn the income they want and deserve. While others that do have the education may not have the will to start all over if they have been down sized. Or maybe they have lost the enthusiasm being in the industry. Some may have just plain and simple selected the wrong industry when they started and might not enjoy it at all. Although that might be the only thing they know how to do, they can always enter into the amazing world of sales.

"Sales people have the opportunity to earn as much as doctors, lawyers professional athletes and even actors and actresses and in many cases, even more"

Chapter 3

A great Sales Persons Finances

This is the chapter that covers the finances of great sales people.

This is the very reason most sales people get into sales to begin with, because of their finances. When most people start a new career in sales their finances are almost always in dire straights. That is one of the main reasons most get started in the sales industry. Some have a lack of finances while others might just be overextended and need additional income for their finances. Some of their finances are completely out of whack and they are in desperate need of a large amount of quick income in order to sustain their lifestyle and are on the verge of loosing everything.

The finances of great sales people are dramatically different than the average or even the above average sales person, but this has not always been the case.

Most great sales people to begin with are not organized people. They great ones have a particular personality that are them naturally or that they have adapted over the years. Either way once they become great they have adapted to and have learned what it takes to be great so by that time they are very different people than when they first began. They have become more motivated, more detail oriented, better organized and have developed good personal finances.

So naturally if someone is not that organized then it would be easy to say that their finances are not in order either. They are busy, busy people that make things happen on a regular basis. They meet many people on a daily basis and focus on the task at hand. While they are making things happen and taking care of their clients and prospecting for new ones, they tend to forget about their personal needs and their personal finances. They tend to start putting their finances off, or sending in some of their payments by the deadline. Eventually they start sending in their payments just a day or too late.

As time goes on and they develop new business and new business clients, they become busier and start making arrangements to pay their bills over the phone. It actually saves them time. They do not have to take the time to write a check, account # and place into the envelope. They also save time by not having to drive to the post office to get their payments mailed out in time.

The problem that arises by paying their bills this way is great sales people tend to prioritize their duties. A great sales person always puts his clients and prospects first. This is very typical with most great sales people and when they prioritize, you better believe that they are going to put their clients and prospects first. They always have someone to call on or someone to see. They also have many deadlines to meet.

This usually means that their bills tend to get last priority. Eventually their bills start getting paid late, and even worse, sometimes they get reported on their credit.

This is a very common situation for many sales people. The great sales people also went through this, but once they have become great they tend to have many more resources than they did when they first got started. So now they may have an assistant pay for their bills, or some one else take care of it for them. But many of the great ones also struggled in this area. The great sales people did not become great by doing one or two things great, they became great by becoming great at many things. Their finances are also one of the things that they learned to be great at.

Great sales people understand the importance of having their finances in order. Having their finances in order they will be able to accomplish more. They will have less to worry about and stress over.

They will not have the fact that they must do something hanging over them. They will be able to focus more clearly at what they do best which is sell and prospect. They also know that when the time presents itself when they will need extra finances to increase their business they will have it available. If they do not have it available they will have the ability to qualify because of their credit in order to get the finances necessary to increase their business.

A sales person's income structure

Great sales people also know that they must have their finances in order in case there is ever a change in their business. Some sales people sell products and serves that are season specific. For instance, when do you think most of a flower shops business comes in? Of course when in season, during the summer season. During this time they will have the majority of their business volume coming in, so it should be obvious that in the winter time their business and sales will most likely be less than in summer.

This is also true for so many industries, ski resorts and everything surrounding it. Snow mobile sales, winter clothing, all terrain vehicle sales, skis, etc. The exact opposite is also true for their counter parts. This would be the summer season, dirt bike sales, summer clothing, bicycles, roller blades, running shoes, sporting goods, etc.

Now this is not only true for seasonal activities, I just wanted to give you the most common scenarios. This is also true for industries. Construction whether it be the construction of new homes or commercial buildings, the construction industry is also dependent on the seasons and they also have a busy season. There are so many different areas and industries related to each of the examples I have given, many more than I have also showed. In construction this will affect electricians, plumbers, dry wallers, carpet sales people, home improvement sales people, landscaping companies, deck builders, painting companies, etc.

The list goes on and on, there are so many industries that are tied to each other. I could give you so many more examples of different types of industries that have busy times, some have nothing to do with the seasons while others do. The fact is, that for many sales people their incomes will fluctuate. There will always be good and better months. As a sales person your income will not be the same consistently and you must adapt to your income structure.

Don't spend what you earn, but as you earn

You must also spend not what you earn, but as you earn.

Retail, in general most retail stores generate about seventy percent of their business during the Christmas season. So most sales people selling retail must realize and take into consideration that they will earn more income during this time. They should not overextend themselves to the point that they might have some struggling times, or not enough income during the slow season to cover all of their finances. This will just add extra unnecessary stress to their personal and business lives. It may also give them a false sense of security over the products or serves they sell. They may indeed earn a great yearly income, but if most of that income comes in during a certain time of year, their expenses unfortunately come in every month of the same year. This means that although they may earn $120,000 per year which divides into $10,000 per month average. They may actually only earn $6,000 the first 6 months of the year and then they may earn $10,000 the 7th and 8th month, and then average $16,000 per month for the last 4 months of the year giving them their $120,000 yearly income.

So in this scenario, if this sales person used the fact that he or she earns $120,000 to qualify for their home, auto and entertainment, this person will indeed struggle the first 6 months of every year. Most peoples homes and autos are amortized over a certain time period and then divided into a certain term. In other words your mortgage payments will be the same amount every month for the entire year. This is also the case for your auto and your monthly expenses. Your liabilities will not take into account that you will have better months than others.

This is a huge factor and one that is overlooked by many sales people and they end up in tough situations that affect their mentality and ability to be at their peak performance. As I mentioned before, it also takes a toll on their mind and they may think they are in the wrong industry because of the up and down months. They may end up making poor decisions based on the way their income is structured, when in reality if they just matched their finances with the way their income is structured, they would have a better quality of life.

Earning more money doesn't mean you'll have more money

It takes a while before learning this basic principle. It is a true fact that when sales people start earning more income they will spend more. Most people in general think that if they earned more they would be able to have more money. The reality is that if they earned more they will spend more according to their new income and not have any extra money at the end of the month.

In other words when someone starts earning more money, they tend to start buying new things. Things they have always wanted if they earned more money. They may start by buying some new furniture for their house. They may also upgrade their automobile since the one they have is already old or it may break down. They may also upgrade their wardrobe. If you have an upgraded wardrobe then it is only reasonable to upgrade your jewelry as well. A new watch, bracelet. Well now that you have upgraded your wardrobe and jewelry, you must also look the part so your hair cuts become more regular and more expensive.

Now you have redefined yourself which is not a bad thing at all. You look and feel better. You are not the same person you were just a couple of years ago when your income first increased. You start wondering why it is you do not have any additional money saved? You have been earning more income for over two years now, and you do not have any additional income saved. This is right around the time you realize that your home is too small for you and does not match who you are. You look, dress and act like the people who live in a lot nicer homes. Also you do not look , drive or act like your neighbors, so you realize you would like to earn even more money so you could upgrade your home. But you just noticed the time and you have no time to ponder that thought since you are meeting some associates for your weekly sales rally at a nice restaurant. It is your fifth luncheon of the week, and it is only Friday.

This is very true. Believe me, I have seen many sales people go through this exact scenario and then wonder why they started sales since they do not have any extra money saved. They get caught up in the moment and do not realize that their quality of life just increased by ten. They do not stop to think about how much money they are actually spending.

Don't get me wrong, I too have been caught up in the same situation, spending all of my new increased income and not realizing that I am spending more than I have ever spent before. I am also not saying spending money is a bad thing. It is the reason we do what we do. It is great to earn a great income and be able to spend it on things that we enjoy.

All I am saying is that you need to realize it and try not to go overboard. In order for you to have your finances in order you must realize this and spend or save accordingly.

Chapter 4

Products and Services

Many people consider these two topics to be the most important when selling or buying. Sales people and consumers alike would consider these to be the most important thing.

I would have to disagree with that point.

Do not get me wrong. I am not saying that product and particular services do not matter. I am simple saying that you can have a large amount of success no matter what your product is or what services you offer.

Sales is sales is sales! It does not matter what you sell. If you like what you sell and believe in it, you can sell a lot of it. As a matter of fact you could sell as much or as little as you would like. It is all up to you and your desires. Well, not all of it. Merely wanting success is not all you would need. You will need to be motivated and willing to do what ever it takes to reach your goals.

Yes, as I said before, you could reach any level of success you would like. And you could sell as much of what ever it is you sell if you want to. Set your goals and you can reach them. Regardless of product or services.

Selling land on the moon

Years ago I read some where about a man who was selling land on the moon! This is a true story and is totally legitimate and legal. If I remember the story correctly, no one had ever filed for rights on the moon here, so he went through the proper channels and was able to obtain some land on the moon that he acquired legally.

Now that he has acquired the land on the moon he began marketing and selling it. Remember this is a true story. He was also able to get millions of dollars of free publicity and there were stories about him in news papers, radio and television shows. If mind serves correctly, I believe he became a millionaire selling land on the moon.

Talk about a tough sale. Think about it. He is selling something that most people cannot use. He is selling something that in no way will benefit his clients. They cannot get anything from it. So why would they buy?

They would buy for many reasons. Maybe even a gag. Just to say they own land on the moon. I would even be willing to bet that each person who has bought this land on the moon display their certificates of ownership. Well, those would be the ones that do not take it so seriously. The ones that take it seriously and are worried what others think would not display it. I'd also be willing to bet that the ones that think they might turn a profit from it would not only not display their certificates, but would hide the fact and not tell anyone about it.

If they announced it, they would most likely be criticized not only by their piers but their family and friends as well. So why would they want to go through this torture.

Can anyone see my point, why buying land on the moon would create some critism and there really is no benefit? Yet people have actually bought it. Also this amazing sales person has also created wealth selling it.

The pet rock

What about that other product? The very successful pet rock? That was also the creation of a super sales person. This amazing sales person was able to invent a product and sold the idea to an industry.

Imagine going a business meeting and trying to sell this idea. I can imagine the looks on the faces of those who listened to him or her. Hey, I have an idea. Why don't we box up some rocks and we can sell them. We can call it the pet rock. It would sell like mad.

I cannot imagine someone agreeing to it from the first visit. But as you would think about it, it would make more and more sense, but as a gag. Which of course it is. Think about it.

Yes, this product is a legitimate product that indeed was very successful and indeed sold millions. I am not sure how much the creator made on this product and I am sure it was a lot. The reason I say this is because if I would have sold this idea, not knowing if it would be successful or not, I would accept almost any reasonable offer. I would probable regret it after seeing the results, but one thing is for sure. The pet rock sold millions of dollars and made millions in profits.

Selling real garbage

I am not sure how many of you remember, but many years ago in the 80's, New York City was having a problem with their trash. They had boat loads of it. Hundreds of thousands of tons that they could not get rid of. They even thought about dumping it in the ocean, but people protested and the boats had to return to New York.

One brilliant and amazing sales person came up with the idea of selling it. What? Are you kidding me, selling New Yorks garbage? That cannot be real, but indeed this is a true story.

Of course they would not just sell it all stinky. They would prepare it, make it pretty, box it up and vuala. There you go.

The idea behind it is that with all of the national publicity and the new publicity it would generate people could have a piece of New York, well it's trash at least.

This too was a successful project and product. I know it sold a lot. I do not have the actual figures and statistics, but I am sure it sold a lot and turned a large profit.

So I do not tell you these stories to impress you how some people are super sellers or amazing sales people. I tell you these stories to impress upon you that products are irrelevant.

A product is a product is a product. You can sell any product.

There is one thing. You must believe in the product. I would bet that each of these people selling these products believed in them. Regardless of what ever anyone else would think or say about them, I would be willing to bet that they would have prepared rebuttals and know exactly how to answer and questions about their products that would make sense. If it didn't make sense it would have never become a reality and no one would have bought it.

If you do not believe in your product, that is okay, but find a new product. I would never recommend to anyone to sell something they did not believe in.

I truly do not think it is worth it regardless of any amount of money.

I would not sell a product I did not believe in. One reason is I do not believe I would have success selling something I do not believe in. I do not care how much selling skills I have, I would not be successful selling something I did not believe in. My clients would see right though me and they would not buy.

Regardless of that, most great super sales people would not sell something they did not believe in. They have more integrity than that. One of the things that make them great and amazing sales people is the fact that they have the ability to persuade people to buy. One way they accomplish this is because they believe in their products so much that they are able to transfer their feelings and emotions of their products to other people who end up buying their products. They see their enthusiasm and then become convinced that they indeed do want to purchase it.

You must believe in your product

You can sell anything to anyone, but choose wisely what products it is you want to sell. This will inevitable have an impact on your success or lack there of.

I have seen some great sales people sometimes not have the success they once experienced or even success they could experience. Sometimes it is simple because of the products they have selected to sell.

Maybe when they first began selling the product they liked it. Maybe they have learned more about the products and now have made some new associations with the product.

What ever the reason one thing is for sure. If they realize it, and they truly do not like or believe in the product, they should stop selling it immediately. That will not benefit anyone. It will not benefit the employer. It will not benefit the sales person. Most importantly it will not benefit the consumer.

How can you sell something to someone when you don't believe in it?

If you do, you would be a hypocrite! You believe one thing and are telling someone something else! You will not last in this business very long. If you do, you will never really achieve the level of success that you could have, had you believed in your product!

Your clients would also never really trust you. They may even buy from you, but never really liking or trusting you. They would leave you with doubts and even negative feelings of you and your company. They will never buy from you again and may never even visit your company again in the future.

Chapter 5

You Must Be Organized

Being disorganized can really have a negative affect in your business and personal lives.

- Managing Paper Piles
- Messy Spaces
- Overcrowded Calendars

One of the things that keep people un organized is clutter.

What is clutter?

Clutter is stuff, it is stuff on the bed, under the bed, in the closet. Clutter is stuff on the desk, under the desk in the drawers, in the closet. It is stuff on the chair, under the chair. Clutter is in the boxes you can't seem to get rid of. Clutter is those magazines that you have held on to but don't seem to read. It is stuff in the car.

How does clutter hurt you?

Clutter beats you in two ways. One way it beats you is physically, you can't get things done if you can't get to it. In other words, if there are things in the way how can you get things done.

Clutter also beats you psychologically.
Imagine this, you just had a great weekend, you are rested and just ready to go! You get to the office and are ready to get things done. When you get to your office, you look at your desk and there's stuff everywhere. It looks like the terminator was looking for something and destroyed everything on it and around it. There is paperwork

everywhere, and you do not have any idea where to begin. That is absolutely devastating to you and it would be to anyone.

So when clutter beats you psychologically it takes a lot out of you mentally. Even if you where ready to go, you must first figure out what things are on your desk. Then once you have come up with a plan of attack, and have executed it. You then must figure out how to deal with or where to put the items on your desk. Some of those items need attention, so you will either deal with them now or later. Some of the items you have discovered are time sensitive and you will end up rearranging your day to deal with those items.

This is just a small example how clutter can beat you psychologically, not to mention the fact that you have rearranged your day and were not able to achieve the level of success you could have, had all of these things been taken care of from the beginning where you could have walked in to an office with no clutter. You could have went right to work and achieved a lot more.

Let's look at the exact flip side of this. You could have had a great day at the office and achieved and accomplished a lot of things. You have gotten things done and you feel very good about yourself and you get home and there is clutter everywhere and it is absolutely devastating.

Clutter is also the stack piles of mail stacked on each other leaning like the tower of pisa.

I know most people including myself stack their mail. They stack their mail until it becomes this huge unmanageable pile of clutter. It grows and grows until it becomes unmanageable. After awhile it is a very unappealing sight. It looks horrible and continues to fall apart and you continue to fix it like it was a game of jenga. Once the stack is to its limit and you cannot stack any additional pieces of mail on it with out the whole thing falling apart, you will look for another spot to start a new mail stack. That very unpleasant pile or piles of mail is no longer just clutter. It has now also now grown into and evolved into a major project. This means that you now cannot just file it away, it has become way too unmanageable and eventually when you get around to it, it is a major project. As a project you will need to invest a lot of time and energy

- **Being neat does not mean being organized**

A good example is and I am sure you have all experienced this before. An important clients or business associate calls you and tells you they are right down the street from your office and would like to speak with you. So all of a sudden you start to cram things everywhere. You make new stacks of stuff, you put stuff in the drawers, you put things all over the place. So when the person gets there the work area looks neat, but it is not organized. Once the person has left, then you end up having to take it all out and trying to reorganize and doing it all over again. So this is essentially doing the same exact work three times. Unless you have a system to follow, you will end up redoing it many more times.

- **An organized person has the ability to find what they want when they want it**

When an unorganized person needs to put something somewhere, he or she asks themselves where do I put this thing.

An organized person would ask themselves where do I find this.

Those are two very important questions you should study and see which category you fall into.

There is a big difference in those two questions.

- **Don't beat yourself up if you are unorganized**

Being unorganized does not mean you are a bad person it just means you have bad systems and have not learned a good system that works for you yet. I have seen many people really beat themselves up from being out of control and not organized. Being unorganized really does affect all areas of your life in a negative fashion. Know that this chapter will help you getting organized and getting rid of stuff. So know that you need a system to help you and apply what you learn. You may have to come back to this chapter several times when reverting to your old ways. Don't get frustrated with yourself, just come back to this chapter and start over.

Paper Clutter

The most common area of clutter comes form paper. Paper, memos, adds, junk mail, important mail, all mail.

Here are some steps that you can take to help get rid of your clutter.

Step One

One thing you should try to do is when opening mail to try and open it over a trash can. This way you will throw away most of the junk mail right then and there before you have a chance to put it somewhere.

Step Two

You can get rid of half of your paper clutter right now and in the future by just throwing away the envelopes and manila folders they came in or where given to you in. Almost all forms of paper clutter came to you in something. Why save the envelopes and such. If there is information you need from the envelope, get that information from it, you can write it right on the back of the paper that was in it and then toss it. That will decrease your paper clutter by half, just by doing that.

You can also decrease your paper clutter by more than half the size by unfolding them. In other words, after you have thrown away the envelopes unfold the paper that was in it. Once you unfold them all you can either file them away or create folders to store them in. Either way you can label them according to what is in it.

I know most people including myself stack their mail. They stack their mail until it becomes this huge unmanageable pile of clutter. It grows and grows until it becomes unmanageable. After awhile it is a very unappealing sight. It looks horrible and continues to fall apart and you continue to fix it like it was a game of jenga. That very unpleasant pile of mail is no longer just clutter. It has now also become a major project. This means that you now cannot just file it away, it has become way too unmanageable and eventually when you get around to it, it is a major project. As a project you will need to invest a lot of time and energy

Step Three

If you cannot throw it away now, then you should have a throw away file or box so you can throw it away in the near future and you still have a place to put it where it is out of the way. This way it will not distract you and have you look at it over and over again which is distracting you through out the day.

Referring items

There are things that will end up on your desk that are not your. Things from other associates that belong to the other associates that you need to act on, do something with, or just look at. These items are not even yours nor did they originate from you, but yet might find their way to your desk.

You should refer these items. You should create some file folders for these types of items that you will file away. This way you can look at it and then also file away. You should not be responsible for other peoples clutter and stuff, but sometimes you will still need to look at those items.

Step One

Create a file folder for each person you will be receiving items from. This way you can have everything in the same place from each of these associates.

Step Two

Create a file folder which each of these other files will be placed together. This way you know where all of them are at, at all times.

Step Three

Create another folder where you would place the items to return to their proper homes once you have done your share with the documents. So you will not have to get up each time you have looked at each of these documents, then you can return to several people all at once on one trip instead of many separate trips.

Take Action

When you are looking at a piece of paper, you should only pick it up once and figure out what needs to happen with it. Who needs to see this? What do I need to do with it? Where can I find it. If there is nothing you need to do with it, then store it away in its proper place. Do not just put it down so that in another half hour you pick it up again and have the same thoughts on what you need to do with it or where it goes. Do not put this piece of paper down so you can pick it up again and again to move it out of the way for another piece of paper. Get rid of it, either trash it, file it or store it away.

Chapter 6

The Consumers

We are all consumers so this chapter will most likely cover some of you reading this. Do not fight it or try deceiving yourself. The more you know about you and what category you fall in or your habits as a consumer will help you understand other consumers with similar habits.

This will obviously help you understand the consumer better which will allow you to help his or her needs better, therefore allowing you the chance to sell them your services or products. This goes both ways. The more the consumer feels comfortable with you and realizes either consciously or sub-consciously that you are meeting their needs (Which you will be) the more the consumer will want to pay for your services or products.

Everyone is a consumer. We all need and purchase services and products to survive. If it were not for the products and services we purchase, we could not survive. For instance, if we didn't purchase the food we eat, we would not exist. Another thing we all need to survive is shelter. We could not survive without shelter. Well we could survive in the right climate, but our existence would be very unpleasant to say the least.

As you can clearly see, there are some things in life that we need for our very survival and existence. We are forced to be consumers by the services and products we need to survive.

Now there are many, many other services and products that we also need. These other services and products may consist of and are not limited to clothing, shoes, eye glasses, medicine, cooking utensils, electricity, running water, etc.

As you can see, these other items and services are not essential for your very survival, meaning you could survive with out it, but your existence would be very unpleasant. Also some of these products are still essential and needed by society. Although you could survive without clothing, society would not allow it. Society has rules and standards that all must follow and society would not allow you or anyone else to walk around butt naked. So these products as mentioned before are also essential for your survival.

These other services and products are not essential for our very survival, but are needed to survive in society.

The Procrastinating Consumer

Consumers are trained to be procrastinators. Just expect it. So long as you know who you are speaking with and are prepared for the simple fact that this is their mode of operation, you should be able to overcome this simple fact.

Do not be alarmed, knowing this simple yet true fact will allow you to be better prepared and will give you the upper hand which you will use to overcome the fact that your prospect is pre-programmed to want to procrastinate.

Why are most people procrastinators?
In reality it is just human nature to hesitate or procrastinate. We are programmed as we grow up through out our entire lives. Our parents, families and friends all share their knowledge with us and try to protect us from what they have gone through or what they have seen or heard of other going through.

It is not that they are mean people, they are just trying their best to help.

Each of us is taught from an early age not to sign anything. Remember that? Okay go ahead and meet with this person, but just do not sign anything until you have talked with me first. Or once, you get the information, do not sign anything until we can call on some of the competitors and we can get a better idea.

So we are taught from when we were just children growing up not to sign things.

What about never buying something on the first meeting? I'm sure you can recall a time when someone may have taught you never to buy something the same day. You must wait until you have had a chance to think about it in order to make a wiser decision. Sleep on it. If not directly said to you, I am sure you have overheard it?

These words are programmed in our nervous system through out the years which is why most consumers are pre programmed to think in this manner. They have been told for many years not to buy things, not to sign anything, to call competitors. Beware of sales people, they get paid to sell you something. Consumers beware, watch out for the small print. Never buy anything over the phone, do not do business with someone you do not know, wait, etc, etc, etc. Yap, yap yap!

Don't get me wrong, yes consumers should be aware who they do business with. But, this way of thinking is out dated and not realistic any longer. As a society we have jumped leaps and bounds and the way technology has also moved, and our economies, there is no way to be an expert at everything. There is no way the average person can call around and have a realistic conversation with a financial planner. There are just too many options to go over.

No way can someone just call a mortgage company and get a rate. A rate for what? Purchase? Refinance? Fixed? Conventional? Conforming? FHA? VA? 15 Year? 30 Year? Points? No Points?

Get the picture, each situation is different. Yes you might be able to call and get some person to give you a rate in that last example, but it does not matter what they say, there is no way you could really know what you are getting whether it is realistic or not? Unless you are an expert in the business or have done a lot of research or have educated yourself, none of it is realistic.

You could get lucky and end up in the right situation at the right time, but most of us don't live using luck. For those of you that do, I don't believe you. If you lived you lives by luck, you would go to Vegas and bet everything you have, just once and double it.

So think about it. Now there are laws when once there wasn't. Businesses have to follow guidelines when years ago they did not. Everything has changed. Don't get me wrong, I'm not suggesting that you be ignorant and trust everyone.

I'm simple suggesting that the companies that are willing to lie to you, will and you will most likely not realize the difference. So yes, you should make sure you know who you are doing business with, but ideas and thoughts that were placed in our head from decades ago might not be the best advice today.

Think about it. As consumers, we are pre programmed this way. How many times have you gone into a retail store looking for a particular item. You know exactly what you are looking for, you are looking for a pair of socks and an associate of the store approaches you and asks, "Can I help you?" Our first instinct and response is almost always, "No thanks, I'm just looking."

What a sad shame, it will take us twice as long to find what we are looking for. We will waste more of our time which should be very important to us, not to mention the fact that we may even have a not so pleasant experience depending on how long it takes us to find what it is we are looking for. Think about it, once we find it, we might then have some questions, and then the associate might be tied up with another client. They might even shy away from you later, because they already asked and got shot down. Some may just now want to seem pesky.

A good sales person will use a rebuttal with you and do his or her duty still and say something like this, "Okay, well my name is Oliver and if you need me, please let me know. But we have some specials at the back of the store, and have a clearance rack there as well. Some of our pants are there and our shirts are there (Pointing)". Then what they have done is still provide you with a good service, and also lower your guard, and now that you feel comfortable, you may actually ask, "well actually I was looking for some socks".

Now all of a sudden, a good sales person has benefited you and his or her employer as well. You are happier and will find what you are looking for and will most likely buy more. A great sales person will do the same, but walk you to what it is you are looking for and see if it is exactly what you wanted. If not a great sales person will also come up with some options and then also try and see if you would like some additional styles and or some shoes to match or even some slacks that go well with it? Accessories.

The point is, why are we trained to say no first? Why is it we would rather take the hard road? Why as consumers won't we just allow someone to help us, especially when it is their job to do so?

Well the answer is pretty simple. There are actually two answers for this situation. One is the simple fact that we also don't want to seem mean and we really do not want to say no if they really do try to sell something to us.

The second is the fact that we as consumers are also a little afraid of buying something, especially since we might feel obligated to buy if they help us. If they show us something, I will feel like I have to buy, even if I don't like it. You should not feel that way.

Instead of consumers being taught things such as;
- Don't sing anything
- Be carefull
- Don't buy the first day

Those things are common sense, well other than the don't sing anything or don't buy the first day. Consumers need to be reprogrammed and trained that it is ok to say no. It is okay for someone to help you and if they cannot meet your expectations not to buy.

If a sales associate helps you and you don't like what they have shown you, you should be able to say, well I was looking for some white socks. I'm really not interested in buying purple ones. Or I wanted some white socks, but these cost more than what I am going to spend. Sales associates understand that. They may even be able to get you what you want, if you just tell them.

So it is okay to get help from a sales associate and not buy if they don't have what you are looking for. It is also okay if someone doesn't want to buy from you if you cannot meet their needs.

So remember, we are all procrastinators to a certain extent. It is because it is human nature and also because we have been pre programmed by our family and friends over the years.

Overcoming the consumers procrastination

Don't think for a second that I think it is okay for a consumer to procrastinate. Remember I am a great sales person and I do not think it is okay for any consumer to wait on a purchase on a product they need or want or service for that matter.

If I do not have the exact product a consumer is looking for, I will already know of something similar. I know the 5 P's though!

Proper Preparation Prevents Poor Performance!

So before I have even showed a product, I know everything there is to know about it. While I am showing the product I am also reading the consumers body language, I study their family, I look at what they look at. Do they look at the price tag first, the quality, color, everything.

I know most consumers will not just tell me exactly what they want or need. After all I am a great sales mane and they know if I know exactly what it is they are looking for that I will sell it to them. You know what? They are right I will and it is okay for me to!

So I will study them, I also know that most consumers do not have the intention to buy the first day. I know they are shopping me. I know they are "PROCRASTINATORS!" I expect it and am very prepared to overcome it. And I won't make the same mistake the last sales guy made by letting them not buy something they need or want.

So as most procrastinators, they also want someone to reassure them that it is okay. And like most consumers they want to know they are not being taken advantage of and that they are getting a good deal. So I give them what they want.

I first meet their needs. If they want white socks, I will get them white socks. If they are looking for this or that I will meet their needs. But their needs also have to be realistic.

When I consulted for mortgage companies, some consumers wanted things that are just not realistic. In many cases even things they did not qualify for. I would train the sales people also known as loan originators in that industry to tell them they could not qualify for that, and showed them how to present it.

Some of the sales associates would tell me, well I use a different approach. I show them how I want to earn their business and work hard at trying to get it for them. Then I let them know after a few days that we could not qualify for that, and that I at least still tried.

That has to be one of the most ignorant things I have ever heard. A sales person working on something that they already know they can't do and also giving false hope to their client. The reason of this sales person is to earn trust. Well, that is exactly what they won't get is their trust. And they better hope I never reach this consumer, because I will make them look like a rookie in my world and the consumer would not only do business with me, but will also school the idiotic sales person. I would have never even presented the wrong program or entertained the fact that I would look into it. As a professional that's what they would pay me to do. Look into it and give them my expertise.

They would love me when I explain why we cannot qualify for what they have asked for, then they would move forward with my suggestions because it makes sense and I have educated them enough for them to feel comfortable moving forward.

My point is, is that just because a consumer wants something, does not mean they can get it and does not mean you can get it for them. So sell what you know you can and it will benefit your clients, yourself and your employer or company.

I already know what consumers also want, so I am always prepared. A consumer wants something for free. They do not want to pay costs and want a product guarantee and also to know that no one else can get them that deal.

They want a low, low interest rate with no closing costs. They want free installation. They want an extended warranty. They want a free upgrade. No points, a free trial membership. Etc, etc.

But in the real world most of what they want is not realistic. I want a billion dollars. So after you listen to what it is they want, don't be surprised, because it is in their nature to want that.

Most importantly what a consumer wants is the thought of maybe being able to get a better deal than what they will end up settling for. They also have the need for the haggle, it makes them feel good. So entertain it, negotiate with them.

If they said they want a ten percent discount now, say, well, I don't think that is possible, but what I can do is give you a gift certificate for $10 off of the next purchase. Or say well I'm not allowed to do that, but I can give you our complimentary, such and such.

If you are in the sales business there is something you could give him or her. Every store has something that they will let clients get away with or give away. Maybe it is an extended warranty. Maybe it is a coupon for $5 dollars off, if you get a good size commission, maybe you pull out a $5 bill from your pocket and buy him a $5 gift certificate.

What ever it is, don't be afraid to go above and beyond. Maybe it is a free delivery. Even though they can fit it in their car, maybe you'll give them a free $10 car loading fee, which is what you would normally charge someone if they were paying you.

Of course that is a joke, and let them know you are joking and that in itself will get them smiling with you and they will appreciate the gesture.

As I have said before we are all sales people, and we should not discourage a consumer to ask. They should ask, and even though they might not get, they should feel good about it, not embarrassed or ashamed to ask. Let them look like the man or the woman in front of their loved ones whom they are trying to impress.

So if someone is not ready to buy right now, you better make sure you know why. Is it the price? Is it the color? Does it not meet their standards? What ever it is, find out and overcome it.

If you cannot find anything, then they are procrastinating and you need to overcome their objection which in this case is their procrastination and nothing they say will be realistic.

For instance, if someone says, well I think it costs too much. You might say something like, these are your basic white socks. The average cost in this state is about $3.99 per pair which is our costs as well. One there is a store right down the street from here who sells the exact same pair, for the exact same price as we do. Believe me, you are not going to get a better deal anywhere. Plus we guarantee the socks and we have a guarantee that you will like it or your money back, so would you just like the one pair or two?

Or if someone says, well I'd like to wait. A great sales person might say, ohh, why is that? When you first came in you seemed very exited that we had the widgets. Why the change of heart?

The great sales person put the ball back in their court. Most people would not expect that, so they might tell you the truth, but will most likely lie. They might say, well I just wanted to see them. Or I heard about it? It really doesn't matter what they say, because both of those are just procrastinating objections.

So you will need to adapt an say something along the lines of, we'll (Name) these just came in and we have already sold out. Or we actually have had such a large amount of requests that these might go pretty soon. We actually had calls on them for the past 4 weeks I'm not even sure if or when we will get them back in. I'd hate to see you miss out on it. You know what (Name)? You can actually buy this tonight take it home to show your family and see what they think. We have a return policy that so long as you don't use it, you can bring it back tomorrow and we will give you a refund, but I'm sure you'll end up keeping it. So was there anything else you needed tonight? Or will this be all?

In both of these situations, the sales person overcame the objection and used the assumptive which we will be covering in detail in a little the book.

Those were all procrastinating objections.

Non procrastinating objections would be objections such as;
- This is too small for my foot
- These sheets are for a queen sized, I have a king size bed

- I wear a size 4-5 this is a size 50
- I wanted a corvette not a cavalier

These are supposed to be funny, but not really. Anything that deals with why they cannot use the product because it does not work for them is not a procrastination objection.

Remember cost should never be used as a reason. If it is something they need and want they will buy, but if you think that is a good enough reason. Then they will buy it from your competitors. Most people shop and look for what they need and can afford. Yes they might not want to spend the money on it, but we have all spent more than we wanted to on something, but we still could afford to do so. If we had it to spend we could afford it.

Don't get me wrong, window shopping is different, I'm referring to serious consumers.

I bet most of you have never test driven a Ferrari! Why not, I bet you love them. Why haven't you? Because you know you might not be able to afford it even to the point that you have probably never even test driven one.

How many of you have put on a $20,000 Rolex? Even when just looking?

How many of you have put a $500 deposit on a $5,000 cruise? Some have and some haven't. The ones that have can afford it. You looked for it, researched it, and acted on it. Then ones that haven't didn't do either and therefore either cannot afford it or are serious enough about not affording it to the point that you would not put yourself in a situation where you might need to make the choice and might end up purchasing something you shouldn't afford but could if you wanted to.

Does that make sense?

Chapter 7

It's A Numbers Game – The Science of Sales

Sales Tracking / Production Sheets

Sales is a numbers game. It does not matter what industry you are in or what you are selling it all boils down to numbers. Every sales person in the world has a mathematical equation to their success or lack there of. Some sales people have a 8-3-2 ratio meaning they need 8 prospects (Leads, Applications, etc) with 3 of them (Pre-Qualified, Approved, etc) granting face to face meetings in which 2 ultimately become new sales. Sales is a numbers game which has been scientifically quantified to know exactly what it takes to achieve ultimate and predictable sales success. I've identified the conversion ratios that clearly describe and reveal the numbers.

Keep in mind that every sales person has a different conversion ratio. Some may be 10-3-1 while others are 5-4-3. The only way to discover exactly what a sales person's conversion ratio is by tracking their prospects, presentations and sales. This procedure is then tracked over a period of time which then reveals the numbers.

The beauty of this is the numbers can be manipulated to generate and reach even the most aggressive sales goals. For the first time ever you will be able to know exactly how many prospects each of your sales persons will need to have in order to reach 5 new sales if that was the goal. Better yet, if you wanted a sales person to reach 5 new sales per week or 5 new sales per day, it does not matter because sales is a science and I've identified the sales conversion code and the Sales Formula. As I said before, sales is a science and as long as you know the sales formula all numbers are attainable!

This scientific method of identifying prospects, qualified and ultimate sales can be duplicated to fit any industry and any sales person or even sales teams.

My sales system is more than just a series of systems and procedures for developing successful sales careers. It is based upon a historical database of over 12 consecutive years of sales activity, production and growth.

My sales system provides sales companies and professionals with a proven scientific road map for success. I've developed what many consider to be the most successful sales system in the world. The production records of the companies and sales people I've worked with and consulted for are some of the highest commissioned sales and conversion ratios in the sales industry.

I've scientifically quantified exactly what it takes to achieve ultimate success in the sales business. We can identify the conversion ratios needed by any one sales professional or sales teams to describe how many prospects, qualified prospects and appointments are needed to reach any sales goal.

This provides the ability to predict, plan and check the activity levels and development of the sales people their goals and objectives.

My system has been tested and proven solid. It is a science! It teaches true fundamentals of selling.

On a daily, weekly and monthly basis, the results of the sales campaign can be reviewed and the levels of success are adjusted to maintain the production goals.

Sales Tracking

The only way any sales campaign can be decided if it was a success or failure is by tracking all of the results involved, not just the actual sales. I'll be including actual examples of the most successful sales tracking (Production Sheets) in the world. You will see how extremely powerful these production sheets are to identify the strengths and weaknesses of the sales campaign. You will also notice how some of the production sheets show exactly how many more prospects and appointments are needed to reach the sales goals.

Production Sheets

I am very pleased to introduce the world to the greatest sales production and tracking sheets in the world.

Oliver P. Maldonado / The Greatest Salesbook in the World

Date		20___ Day	20___ Projected
Date			

Customer Name	Lead Generator	Appt Setter	Mtg Director	Lead Source	Loan Amount	Appraisal	Credit Repr	Resolution	Date	State
New Client 114	Generator 1	Appt Setter 2	Director 1	Tele	$164,000.00	$300.00	$65.00			Mkt 2
New Client 115	Generator 2	Appt Setter 1	Director 1	Tele	$122,000.00	$300.00	$0.00			Mkt 2
New Client 116	Generator 3	Appt Setter 1	Director 3	Tele	$215,000.00	$0.00	$65.00			Mkt 3
New Client 117	Generator 4	Appt Setter 2	Director 2	Tele	$170,000.00	$300.00	$65.00			Mkt 4
New Client 118	Generator 2	Appt Setter 2	Director 4	Tele	$217,000.00	$300.00	$65.00			Mkt 4
New Client 119	Generator 1	Appt Setter 2	Director 3	Referral	$472,000.00	$300.00	$65.00			Mkt 3

Totals	To Date $	$19,161,321.00	Today	$1,360,000.00 To Date	$1,500.00 To Date	$325.00 Appt via social 238%	$3,665.00

Confirmation Rate

Leads

	App vs. Seen 32%				Leads with Socials 19	Daily Average 19	
	Today	To Date	Daily Average	Projected	To Date 380	Projected 380	
Total Leads	8	603	30.15	603			
Appointments	28	584	29.20	584.00	Average Loan		
Double Leads	22	438	21.90	438.00	$ 161,019.5		
Seen	7	289	14.45	269.00	Seen Today	Seen To Date	To Date %
Sold	4	117	5.85	-117.00	1	13	38.46%
Clearing Ratio	57.14%	40.48%	40.48%	40.5%	0	38	60.53%
Loan Volume	$1,360,000.00	$19,161,321.00	$923,616.00	$19,161,321.00	0	25	64.00%
Director 1	1	5	0.25	5	2	41	58.54%
Director 2	0	23	1.15	23	0	1	2800.00%
Director 3	0	16	0.80	16	1	43	39.53%
Director 4	0	24	1.20	24	1	22	45.45%
Director 5	0	28	1.40	28			
Director 6	1	17	0.85	17			
Director 7	0	10	0.50	10			

Marketing Sources

	Today	To Date	Average	Projected
Market 1	20	224	11.20	224.00
Market 2	2	73	3.65	73.00
Market 3	12	295	14.75	295.00
Market 4	17	255	12.75	255.00
Market 2	1	33	1.65	33.00
Market 3	8	246	12.30	246.00
Market 4	5	209	10.45	209.00
Market 1	6	145	7.25	145.00
Market 2	2	11	0.55	11.00
Market 3	1	38	1.90	38.00
Market 4	0	36	1.80	36.00
Market 3	1	24	1.20	24.00

Appointments by Setter

	Appt Setter 1	Appt Setter 2	Appt Setter 3	Appt Setter 4	Setter 1	Setter 2	Setter 3	Setter 4	Setter 5	Other
Today	9	12	0	0	2	2	0	0	0	0
To Date	315	315	1	12	52	57	0.00	0.05	0.00	0.05
Average	14.75	15.75	0.05	0.60	2.60	2.85	0	1	0	1
Projected	295	315	1	12	52	57				

Leads Generated

Date	Generator 1	Generator 2	Generator 3	Generator 4	Generator 5	Generator 6	Gnrtr 7	Gnrtr 8	Gnrtr 9	Gnrtr 10
Lead Generator										
Today	0.0	9.0	0.0	0.0	8.0	5.0	7.0	9.0	5.0	0.0
To Date	96.0	154.0	112.0	8.0	93.0	101.0	97.0	143.0	42.0	6.0
Average	4.80	7.70	5.60	0.40	4.85	5.05	4.85	7.15	2.10	0.30
Projected	96.0	154.0	112.0	8.0	93.0	101.0	97.0	143.0	42.0	6.0

Signoff's / Sign offs from Appt. Setters

Date	Lead Generator	Generator 2	Generator 3	Generator 4	Generator 5	Generator 6	Gnrtr 7	Gnrtr 8	Gnrtr 9		Today %	To Date %
Today	9.0	0.0	0.0	0.0	11.0	13.0	7.0	13.0	6.0	Today	100.00%	38.46%
To Date	11.0	24.0	8.0	0.0	11.0	13.0	0.55	0.80	16.0	To Date	#DIV/0!	60.53%
Average	0.45	1.20	0.40	0.05	0.55	0.65	4.85	0.80	0.30	Average	#DIV/0!	64.00%
Projected	9.0	24.0	8.0	1.0	11.0	13.0	11.0	16.0	6.0	Projected	#DIV/0!	58.54%
											#DIV/0!	2800.00%
											100.00%	39.53%
											#DIV/0!	45.45%

Referrals

	Market 1	Market 2	Market 3
	0.00	1.00	0.00
	0.00	2.00	3.00
	0.20	0.10	0.15
	4.0	2.10	3.15

TheGreatestSalesbookinTheWorld.com

I'm not sure how the actual copy of one of my daily production sheets will ultimately look? So if you cannot read very well, I'll explain some of what is contained in it.

Also keep in mind that the daily production sheets I use have evolved over years of manipulating the #'s and adding and subtracting the #'s we didn't need. In other words, if I decided I needed to know how many leads or prospects each of my sales people got on a daily basis, I would add that. If I needed to also know how many he/she had in a weekly and monthly basis, I would ad that as well. If I thought I no longer needed to know how many they had for a 2 month period I would eliminate that from the production sheets. Keep in mind that you can create your own production sheets. I actually provide these sheets and templates of them to the clients I consult with. I also have these templates available for sale which you can get from www.TheGreatestSalesBookintheWorld.com

A daily production sheet should have a beginning date and an end date, meaning that the production period is based on a certain amount of sales. My daily production sheets are based on 20 selling days, so I have 12 selling campaigns per year. I would not recommend doing a one year production period, in my opinion the #'a are too hard to control and you have a lot more room for error. On a monthly campaign, you can adjust an individual salespersons #'s on a daily or weekly basis to achieve your goals. You will also be able to adjust the campaign to reach all #'s. If you like you can have a separate management yearly production sheet that would indeed be based on 12 months in order to manage the managers and their teams.

So let me get down to my #'s. These are actual #'s from one of my actual daily production reports which was done in one month of 2003.

Day 20 of 20 selling days.

Today Gross Sales:	$1,360,000.0
Total Gross Sales:	$19,161,321.0
Daily Average:	$ 923,611.0
Total New Units:	119
Daily New Units Average:	5.95
Total New Leads:	603
New Leads Daily Average:	30.15
Total Qualified:	483
Total Seen:	289
Top Salesperson:	28 Units
Top Sales Daily Avg:	1.4 Units
Top Sales Conv. Ratio:	88%
Top Lead Generator:	154 Leads
Daily Average:	7.70 Leads

This should give you an idea of my daily production and tracking reports. This is just a small amount of information that each one of my daily productions sheets gives me. My daily production sheets have each of my lead generators information on a daily / to date / projected average, along with each of my salespeople, each of my markets, total production for all and individual, daily average for all and individual, etc.

Track what you expect!

If you are a sales manager, business owner, or salesperson and you don't track your leads, appointments, presentations, sales, then you will never really hit the numbers you've only dreamed of. If you don't track your numbers you will never even really be able to set an actual goal? You won't know what your goal should be or could be? How could you know if you have no idea how many people you could see? Or how many leads you have or average on a daily basis?

Tracking and knowing your numbers is in actuality the most important part of all sales. Without proper tracking you'll never reach your true potential. I know some of you might say, but you've hit one of your goals? Well, that would be a shame, because that happened through luck and sales is a science. For those of you who have hit one of your goals, let me ask you, was that one month out of the year? So that would make your hit ratio was 1/12. That is merely a 8.33% hit ratio and no one can survive on those numbers? The ones that can will live a mediocre life and have mediocre income and the company unfortunately will never see their true potential!

If you are an individual salesperson reading this and your sales manager does not have a tracking system in place, then you should start one of your own. Don't wait until someone else gets around to it someday. Someday never comes. Don't let someone else control your destiny and your life. I challenge you to control your own destiny and your own life!

I guarantee you that if you start tracking on a simple basis, just track your daily, weekly, monthly leads.

Then track your daily, weekly, monthly appointments.

Then track your daily, weekly, monthly sales.

Then divide each into itself and you'll have all of your ratios. You'll know exactly how many more leads and appointments you need to reach what ever your sales goals are!

Go for it! Mind your business, because no one else will!

Do You Know Your Number's?

It never surprises me how many companies and salespeople have no idea what their numbers are. This is a sure way to fail. How can anyone reach their goals if they do not know what their numbers are? If they do not know what their conversion ratios are, how can any company or sales person know how many more prospects they need and need to see to hit their daily, weekly and monthly goal? It is virtually impossible to predict with out using a scientific approach such as daily production sheets.

If you want to be a successful sales person you must track and know your numbers!

If you want to run a successful sales team, you must track and know all of your sales persons numbers and also track and know your entire sales teams numbers. You must also take it a step further and meet with each sales person individually and as a team and make sure they know their numbers.

If you are wondering why in the world a sales manager or sales person would not track or know their numbers the answer is simple. The reason is because of fear and embarrassment. No one wants to know they are not producing at their peak or ability. Sales people do not want to know they are under producing, even though they already know, they just do not know exactly by how much. Sales managers are the same. But trust me, you will never ever reach or even know your true potential or have your sales teams reach their potential if you do not know your numbers.

Winners track their numbers, losers don't want to know.

Tracking your numbers is so important in so many ways that I want to go over a few.

Tracking and knowing your numbers will;

- Identify your strengths
- Identify your weaknesses
- Identify what is needed to reach goals
- Project what you can expect
- Holds the sales Manager and Sales People Accountable

These are just a few important reasons to track your sales and your teams sales.

I cannot stress it enough how important it is to track your results so I'll issue all sales people and sales managers a challenge. I challenge all of you to track your results and see if you do not increase your results every month after you've begun tracking your numbers.

To all of you that do not track your numbers, know that you are scared. It is okay to be scared and this fear can propel you to newer heights. Those sales people and sales managers that do not track their numbers are doomed to a sales life of mediocrity and never reaching their true potential or the potential of their sales team.

"Winners track their numbers, losers don't want to know"

Chapter 8

Communication

Communication is a very important skill all sales people must master. Great sales people have mastered this skill very well. I should not be referring to communication as a skill; it is more like an art form. If you can think back in time try and remember all of the most influential people you can remember, dead or alive. I can almost guarantee you they were great communicators and chose the words they used very wisely.

All great leaders, business people, of all walks of life and backgrounds, the ones that were most memorable in a positive light were the great communicators. Think back to a John F. Kennedy. What did he say? "Ask not what your country can do for you, but what you can do for your country!". He has not been around for many, many years, but we can still remember what he said and the words he used. It does not matter that he has been dead for so long or that there is a whole new generation that was not even alive when he made that speech, yet many people remember his words.

How about a Martin Luther King? What did he say? "I have a dream", it is the same thing, he was a great communicator and selected very powerful words to communicate with. Although he has not been around for many years, we can still remember his powerful and moving words.

That is the power of communication and words the great leaders are remembered throughout time. Great communicators are also great sales people and great leaders. To be totally correct, great communicators are great at what ever they set their mind at doing, primarily because they can almost always achieve what ever it is with their great communications skills. Great communicators have the great ability to influence and lead people. That in itself is a very powerful thing to be able to do. Don't just take my word for it, let me give you an example. One of the first Americans to earn over one Million dollars per year was Charles Schwab. Charles Schwab was given an annual salary of at least One Million to be president of United States Steel Company in 1921. Charles has even admitted that there were several people who worked for him that knew a lot more about steel and the production of steel than he did, so then why would they pay him this large amount of money during a time when seventy five dollars per week would have been considered upper middle class? It wasn't for his brilliance, there were many other people during that time that were a lot more brilliant than he was. It wasn't that he knew more about steel and the production of steel than anyone else, he personally admitted that there were others that knew more. The simple fact by his own admission was that he was mostly paid this large sum of money for his ability to deal with people. In other words he was able to communicate and deal with people better than anyone else and that was worth over one million to the United States Steel Company at the time. He also said the greatest asset he possessed was his ability to generate enthusiasm among his people!

Think about that for a moment?

It is obvious that he was correct! Not only during that time but in today's time as well. Great communicators who also use powerful words are worth their weight ion gold, not only because they can communicate well with others, but the affect their communication has on others.

In my mind great communicators are also great sales people even if they are not selling any products or services, they are in the business of influencing people to do what they want, and that in my mind is called selling. That brings us back to great sales people. Great sales people that have mastered the art of communication will obviously convert more sales than others; they will achieve higher levels of success than normal because of their great communication skills.

Don't be fooled about communication, great communication is not enough. Just because someone is a great communicator does not mean that, that's all it takes. The great communicators are also great persuaders. They persuade people a lot more than most people also because of the fact that they can communicate well, so they can always make something sound great. They also say things that even when someone is not interested in what it is they might be saying or even if the other party has a different opinion, they can change the conversation around and readjust their communication in order to get their point across that will influence the person they are communicating with.

Become a master at communicating with people and watch how you'll all of a sudden be able to influence so many people as if using magic or placing a spell on them.

Communication by Script

Great communicators also have pre-scripted material, many of them keep it in their head, but it's scripted none the less.

Most if not all great sales people also use this form of communication, which has been pre-scripted for them. Trust me not all great sales people have the natural ability to communicate well with everyone, but if they have already mastered a presentation along with their rebuttals then of course the communication they will have with others will seem as if they are a great communicator.

Many sales people I have worked with and trained for many years were not all great communicators, heck a large majority did not have an education, me included. But as long as I made sure all of my sales people mastered their presentations and rebuttals, along with a lot of role playing, I can assure you when they talked about their products and services, they communicated extremely well. The reason was because everything was scripted for them. They really didn't even have to think, they just had to follow their presentation which also included small talk, and then they had to answer any objections or questions with pre-scripted answers.

In the mortgage industry I really never even educated my sales people on the mortgage industry. I trained them with some basic product knowledge and everything else was scripted. They did not need to know how a mortgage is done, so long as they new how to explain the mortgage. I had other more analytical people figuring out the mortgages and the pre-approvals, and I just wanted the sales people to go out and explain that they have been pre-approved and that they can guarantee their mortgage payments, savings and closing costs as we're showing them.

I've had mortgage sales people literally coming into the business and only knowing what I have taught them in a week or two have clients call me and tell me how knowledgeable my sales person was and how the last few companies and sales people they have met with could not even explain their mortgage like that. I can't recall how many times I've heard that. I've also had many clients tell me how they've learned so much from this person and they were happy to work with someone so experienced, many times just a week or two of experience, and they are schooling someone who has done many mortgages in their life.

I can remember one of my new mortgage sales people several years ago came back with a sign off (Sale) with a pretty large mortgage. He had collected all of the documentation required, along with a check for $365 paying for the appraisal and credit report. It was not that surprising since we did a ton of business like this all day long, what was surprising was the fact that the new client was the president of a chain of banks who also did mortgages. This person ran 10 branches and we knew exactly who he was. Many in the office thought it was a joke, some thought he was trying to spy on us. I looked it over and we didn't lower any fees or costs for this seasoned veteran.

We charged him the exact amount we would charge anyone. We collected 100% of his original documentation, tax returns, pay-stubs, banks statements, mortgage statements, everything. I had no doubt that this was totally legit, bus since the company I was consulting for had never seen our work, they had a large amount of doubt and wanted me to check it out with the client. I refused. Not that I had a problem speaking with a client or sales person, but not when everything is exactly how we've asked for it. As far as I was concerned it was ok.

The company actually had the nerve to say they would not proceed with the processing of the mortgage. I met with the owner and assured him that everything is in order and if they had any concerns about the intentions with the borrower they were unfounded and it was not like we were working or teaching him our secrets even if he was a spy. We were just doing a loan for him and will earn a profit from him.

To make a long story short, everyone in the office was taking bets if the loan would even go through. I also had the 2nd partner of the organization ask us about our client, I assured him as well that everything is the way it is supposed to be.

I was becoming a little concerned myself, but not about loosing the sale, but by the reasoning behind someone that can do a loan, not using his own resources. I decided to close the loan myself, just so I could ask the client.

I met with the client, everything on this loan went very well. The client had great credit, great income and was very organized. After I closed his loan, which we were saving him quite a bit of money on his refinance. I asked, and he answered. Although his banks did mortgages, they did not specialize in them. He could do a mortgage with his banks, but quite frankly we were the specialists and were able to get him a mortgage not just a little better than the one he could do with his banks but way better. Better closing costs with a lower interest rate and a better program for him, so it would be foolish for him to do it with his banks, especially since that is not what they specialize in.

That was that. It made sense, we were saving him a ton of money every month, and when I looked at his last mortgage company, his banks, he was right. That's one of the reasons how we were also able to save him so much money, he was not in the best program possible and we were the specialists and we did him a great service.

Everyone was shocked, it was a win-win situation for the client and us. It was also one of the most profitable mortgages of the year, so that was an added bonus.

Wouldn't you know, just a few weeks later this same sales person came back to the office with a new sign off (Sale) and this time it was for the mayors son. Once again we went through the same doubt, but this time no one was willing to look foolish enough and question whether the mortgage would go through or not.

These examples are just to show you that with the proper communication you'll be able to communicate with anyone including those that are very savvy and know what they are talking about and also hearing. I'm sure that had some other inexperienced sales person met with the bank president or mayors son, neither would have done business with them. But a new sales person with the right type of communication can achieve the end result. Now imagine a seasoned sales person with the right communication skills, they should never loose another sale.

Communication is not only about talking

There is a lot more about communicating with someone than just speaking. How you dress communicates to the prospect or client about you before you even have a chance to open your mouth. Your grooming also speaks a low about you, before you even say a word to the person you will be communicating with. So don't be fooled into thinking that talking alone is enough, communicating is much more than just talking.

When you are communicating with someone, always look them in the eyes.

Let this be a lesson to you. You should treat everyone the same way, and if you communicate good enough with them, you'll be surprised who you'll be able to do business with.

Vocabulary

The power of words. Words are the most powerful thing that has ever been developed on the planet. With out words the light bulb could have never been invented. Neither would the telephone for that matter. We as humans have made it to the top of the food chain because of our ability to use words and communicate with each other.

Words can be used for greatness or misery. Words can make you laugh while others will make you cry. Words have destroyed countries and at the same time united nations!

Words are the only way a Gandi could have lead millions of people to peace while absorbing a large amount of punishment and violence.

The great and holy Dalai lama also used very powerful words to lead and inspire a great many people.

Since words have this kind of power it would be unwise to think that words have only been used for greatness, words have also been used for devastating destruction by people such as Adolph Hitler. Hitler's words were used to lead his followers to do horrible unspeakable things to man kind. Words have also been used for mass destruction by people such as Osama Bin Laden.

As you can clearly see, words can be used for hope and all that is good for man kind or words can also be used for mass destruction and devastation.

The great thing is we all have the great resource of words and vocabulary to use. No one is limited to which words they can or cannot use. In America that is one of our greatest assets, freedom of speech is our constitutional right.

We all have the ability to communicate as we choose and it does not matter what your background, education or up raising was or is. Those things have only impacted the words you have been subjected to, but you can go to any library or bookstore and find a number of great books on communication and vocabulary. You can pick up one of the most famous books on words known as the English dictionary. I encourage everyone to read the dictionary and start right in the beginning and start reading. You'll soon start realizing you use a very small amount of words on a daily basis. As you read, you'll also discover that of the words you do read, you really don't know the definitions on a lot of words you may have heard. As you read the English dictionary, you'll also start reading words in the definitions themselves that you do not understand and will find yourself looking up new words to learn what those new words mean. Before you know it, you'll start using an assortment of new words in your daily vocabulary.

The English language consists of over 500,000 words and has the most words of any other language. That being said it is amazing how the average person uses only about 2,500 to 10,000 words. This means we use less than 3% of the total English language. That's a shocking truth.

One of the greatest books and the one I've personally recommended most is by Anthony Robbins titled "Awaken the Giant

Within". If you haven't read that book yet, I strongly encourage you to pick it up. It can change your life if you read it. In his book there is a section on vocabulary and Anthony Robbins mentions how William Shakespeare used over 24,000 words in his works. Of those 5,000 words were only used once. That's amazing! Think about how many millions of people have been influenced one way or another from his works. How many movies and theatre have been done from his words. His words and the meanings of his words have been studied in high schools and colleges around the world! That is powerful! Also think about the fact that even though he used so many more words than most, he still used a small portion from the entire language and had much more of an impact than most.

Choose your Words Wisely

You words you select to use on a daily basis can and will have an effect on others. You can choose what effect that is whether a positive or negative effect.

Try not to only choose words that are different or that some may not have heard, try to select words to include in your daily vocabulary that can have a positive effect on peoples lives.

Most people have or use more negative words to communicate with. I have also found that there are more negative words available than there are positive. From some of my research, I've discovered that there are only about thirty one out of every three words are positive ones.

I've personally changed a lot of my vocabulary and the words I consistently use to communicate with others and I have complied a list here of positive and negative words you can start using immediately. You can use some of them or all of them to start with. I encourage you to learn some of your own that you can consistently use with your daily communication.

Here are some positive words you can start using immediately with your vocabulary.

Positive words

Fantastic	Great	Amazing	Incredible	Adoring
Good	Positive	Increase	Enthusiastic	Influence
Success	Talent	Energetic	Animated	Ideas
Admire	Optimum	Can	Will	Beautiful
Performance	Idea	Strategy	Imagine	Cherish
Frugal	Imagine	Creative	Enormous	Massive
Incredible	Illusive	Wonderful	Best	Terrific
Monumental	Historic	Awesome	Excellent	
Absolutely	Creative	Spectacular	Fabulous	
Adore	Exceptional	Super	Willful	
Determined	Extraordinary	Persistent	Negotiated	
Consistent	Flattering	Understand	Understated	
Familiar	Appreciate	Ultimate	Remarkable	
Marvelous	Special	Stupendous	Surprise	
Phenomenal	Outstanding	Income	Money	
Project	Talent	Supernatural	Miracle	

Doing	Done	Correct	Example
Selective	Marvelous	Believe	Astonishing
Breathtaking	Win	Won	Impressive
Stunning	Striking	Expected	Ready
Prepared	Skilful	Gifted	Natural
Unbelievable	Superb	Remarkable	Superior
Electrifying	Greatest	Miraculous	Victory
Victorious	Achieve	Achievement	Titanic
Successful	Dynamic	Thrilling	Exciting
Dazzling	Completed	Superstar	Abundant
Tremendous	Strong	Team	Exhilarated
Honor	Distinguished	Admirable	Tremendous

Negative words

Sustainable	Input	Brain Storming	Suggestion
Extreme	Eccentric	Ridiculous	Ludicrous
Irrational	Nonsensical	Outlandish	Peculiar
Odd	Foolish	Fictional	Extravagant
Excessive	Overwhelming		Unlikely

Bizarre	Unrealistic	Negative	Eerie
Speculative	Illusive	False	Exaggerated
Melodramatic		Fabricated	Embellished
Overstated	Ordinary	Strained	Excessive
Extravagant	Distorted	Overstated	Inconceivable
Ego	Unprecedented		Unthinkable
Outrageous	Unbelievable	Dramatic	Defeat
Conspicuous			

Chapter 9

Having a Great Attitude

Attitude! Many say that attitude is everything, and I for one would agree with that. I would like to clarify however that attitude alone will not make a great sales person. This has been a misconception many have had for many years. Yes it is great to have a great attitude and be confident, but people tend to associate these characteristics with sales people. I should clarify a little more, since great sales people tend to have these characteristics they stick in peoples minds. Since most people like great sales people and one of the things they remember the most of these sales people is how they acted and how confident they were. In their mind that is why they bought from them.

They did not realize that the great sales person was a highly trained finely tuned athlete. The great sales person did their job and since they are great they made it look easy.

So a great attitude is very important and essential but it is not everything and is not all that is needed to be a great sales person.

In the world of sales and marketing a great attitude is essential. In our world there is so much negativity already that it is easy to get caught up with negative feelings and emotions that will in fact hurt the way we sell. This is a fact. If we begin to feel negative it will affect the way we communicate and communicating is how we sell. If we communicate improperly our prospects will see it and not buy. Even if they do not realize it and or know we are feeling negative they can sense it and will not buy.

A sales person deals with more negative situations in one day than the average person deals with in an entire month or even an entire year. Sales people do not only deal with negativity from their prospects but from everyone. A sales person deals with their managers who are always demanding more.

A great sales person also deals with their managers not only because of production, quotas and goals but also to try and provide better products and services for a lower cost. A great sales person also knows that by having better products and services available will also increase their sales. They are great sales people and already know they could sell any product, so now imagine that they also have better products. They know they will sell more of the better products. If they have better service, they know they will be able to sell more of the better services also. If they have both, they will sell more of both.

That is not the only reason great sales people want better services and products, another reason is because it makes their lives and jobs easier. Great sales people try to keep things as simple as possible. So if they have better services and products they will have an easier time explaining and selling.

One of the most important reasons great sales people want and fight for better products and services is mainly because of their clients. They will have less client complaints and happier clients. This is great for their clients. It will also get them more repeat sales and referrals which as we have already said leads to more sales. This is a win-win- win situation for everyone, the consumer, sales person and company.

This is getting off of the topic a little bit, but it is very important to know and understand what great sales people think. So as I was saying great sales people are constantly dealing with negative situations and people. They fight many battles, battles that are rarely seen by the general public and they are always selling.

They sell the company owners on products and services, their retailers for this or that and the list goes on and on. As I said, they deal with more negative people and situations than the average person does so in order for them to be productive and get the results they want, they must maintain a great attitude.

This attitude must show with all of the areas of business they deal with. With a positive attitude a great sales person can achieve anything in any situation.

It is inevitable that there are not only going to be negative people you will have to deal with. It is also inevitable that there will be many more negative situations you must deal with, so since you have to deal with these people and situations already why not have a great attitude about it and turn the negative people and situations into positive ones.

A great attitude is infectious. It will rub off on everyone you are in contact with. More people will want to be around you. Other sales people will want to be in your presence and your clients will not want you to leave when you are done.

The bottom line is a great attitude will enhance your life. With a great attitude you will have more fun. People around you will have more fun. Your life, family, friends and clients will also all benefit from your great attitude.

Great sales people know how to turn it on and off, but it has taken many years and hundreds if not thousands of presentations to learn how.

Great sales people have rituals they follow to help keep them with a great attitude. It should be obvious however that great sales people work and use everything available to them in order to maintain a great attitude because they know a great attitude is not enough.

Things to help your attitude

Great sales people read positive material. They read a lot of self help and motivational books. They apply what they read. They have goals, they write them down and read them often. They keep track of their numbers. They work on their weaknesses.

They use music to help their state of mind. Think about it, have you ever heard a song that just made you feel good? Is there a favorite song you have even one that you may not have heard in a long time that just makes you feel good? Great sales people do also and a lot of them will use these songs to help their state of mind. They will listen to these songs and it will motivate them.

They will also listen to motivational tapes in their cars while driving to appointments with their clients.

Dress for your attitude

Great sales people also dress in ways that make them feel good about themselves which also help their attitudes. They have favorite shirts, ties, suits, and cuff links and such to help their attitudes.

"The bottom line is a great attitude will enhance your life, and the lives of people around you"

Chapter 10

Overcoming the fear of REJECTION

Fear of rejection is one thing that most people getting into the sales industry go through. Yes you heard it right. Fear of rejection is very real for a lot of people getting into the sales industry but even veterans that have forgotten the basics go through this fear.

Why do sales people have this fear?

I have said it all through out this book and have preached it for many years to the thousands of sales people I have trained. A sales person will go through more rejection in one day than most people will face in an entire month and depending on the type of sales maybe even an entire year.

No one wants to be rejected in any way shape or form. It does not matter what you are selling or even in your personal life, most people fear rejection. That is why most people will avoid doing things where they may get rejected. Think about it, most people do not approach people they might feel an attraction to because of fear of rejection. Most people have not applied for the jobs they have really wanted because of fear of rejection. Most people also do not ask for things because of the same fear. Although you might want a discount on something at a store, most will not ask for it, for the simple fear of rejection.

No one wants to get rejected it hurts our egos and make us feel bad. The one thing that comes along with all sales is rejection. Rejection is inevitable when selling. It does not matter what you are selling. It could be services, products. It could be something someone desperately needs or not. It could be the most inexpensive product or service available rejection is still inevitable. You could even give something away and you would still get rejected. You should embrace and expect the rejection.

Try to imagine any other industry or job where there is so much rejection. I cannot imagine another industry. It is part of the game and everyone who enters the business of selling should embrace it.

How Great Sales People Avoid Rejection

The greatest sales people in the world also have rejection but they do not fear it. They expect it. They embrace it, but they do not like it. Imagine a sales person so great that he does not encounter any rejection in years.

Well I guess it depends on what your definition on rejection is?

For instance, if your definition of rejection objections, then this would not be the case in this example. It would be virtually impossible not to be rejected in years. Now if your definition of rejection is not getting the sale, this is the type of rejection I am referring to. I know of great sales people including myself that have closed one hundred percent (100%) of the people they have met with in years. Yes that is right, imagine some great sales people not loosing a single sale in many years. Going one hundred percent (100%). Most people think that is unimaginable, but it is very real. I know of many great sales people including myself who have gone many years without loosing a single sale.

Does that mean these great sales people have not encountered rejection? Of course they have encountered objections that could have easily turned into rejection but they have overcome the objections and turned them into a closed sale. Some of these sales people I am referring to do not just see a few people a month. I am referring to those as well, but that does not impress me much. I am referring to the great sales people who meet with several people per day that have not lost a sale.

Years ago when I used to travel this great country of ours setting up sales and marketing offices for other companies, I would meet with several business owners per day on my recruiting trips. Once my promotion was set up and started, I would meet with from anywhere between eight to twelve (8-12) clients per day sic days per week. I have gone many, many months closing one hundred percent (100%) of everyone I met with whether a business owner or regular consumer. I closed one hundred percent of the people I met with for many months at a time. My overall yearly closing or conversion ratios were always in the ninety percentile (90%). Yes that means that for the entire year I closed or converted over ninety percent (90%) of all the people I met with for the entire year.

Those numbers are very real and realistic. I tracked my performance for many years and the performance of my promotions. I also tracked the numbers of my sales people. So I know these numbers are not just because I am some great sales person, although I am, I have created many sales scripts, presentations and the like that were extremely successful. I have trained many people that have never sold a thing who have also closed and converted at these high ratios. I have learned over time that anyone following a good system can also close at these high ratios.

I will be including examples of the actual scripts and sales presentations that I have used over the years and ones that I have also trained others to use in this book.

So how is this possible?

How can I avoid rejection like these great sales people?

Well the answer is simple! I call them the 5 P's.

Proper Preparation Prevents Poor Performance!!

Master these 5 P's and you too will avoid rejection. Don't get me wrong, rejection is a necessary part of the sales industry and is unavoidable. It is present and will be present the entire time you are in the sales industry.

So you will really never completely avoid rejection all together, but you will be able to reduce the amount of rejection you encounter by using the 5 P's. By being properly prepared you will prevent poor performance!

How else do you think someone could consistently close one hundred percent (100%) of the people they see. How could great sales people close or convert over nincty percent (90%) of everyone they meet with for years at a time?

If you thought great sales people closed at those high ratios just because they were likeable or flamboyant, you would have been extremely mistaken. Great sales people close at such high conversion ratios for the very simple fact that they are very prepared. They have role played their sales presentations, know all of their rebuttals are persistent and always give their best. They know their products and services better than anyone else including their superiors. They also know the products and services of their competition better than their competitors themselves.

This is how they convert at such high ratios. This is the only way they or anyone else can convert at such astounding ratios.

Great sales people also do not like rejection, they don't like it so much that they have made themselves experts at what they do. They have spent countless hours mastering their sales presentations and role playing with their team mates until they can anticipate what the clients or prospects will say before they say it.

This is how they can dramatically reduce the amount of rejection they encounter.

So if you fear rejection and want to encounter less of it. Master the 5 P's. Learn your products and services better than anyone else. Master your sales scripts, presentations and rebuttals. Role play, role play until you feel so confident and can answer any and all questions anyone could possible ask you regarding your products and services and you too will begin closing at a higher ratio than you ever thought possible. You too will start experiencing less and less rejection.

Don't just take my word for it, try it for yourself and attempt to prove me wrong. Keep in mind that I have practiced what I preach and have trained thousands of successful people over the years all around our country.

Do not just try to master your sales presentations while working, take it home. Read it to yourself over and over again. Make notes about it. Record yourself reading it. Role play with your family, friends, co workers. Overcome their objections over and over again. Continue doing this. It may take many days or weeks or even months, but the experience you will get by doing this will be invaluable. It will increase your results dramatically. Your results will grow at a higher level than anyone could have ever expected including yourself.

Do not just do this for the moment. In other words, do not just do it for right now. You will have to also create and adapt to the changing times, economies, people and products. Even if you sell but only one product, that product will get better and better. They're will be modifications on the product and such. If you sell services, your services along with the services of your company will change as they adapt with the needs of their changing clients or competition.

As your company ads new products and services, you should master them right away. It will help you and your clients. You will actually start to notice that other sales associates including the managing staff in your company will start to look at you as the expert and will then begin coming to you for the answers. This is not a bad thing. You will end up with more sales and referrals because of it.

Each time a sales person has a sales call they do not think they could handle, they will end up calling on you. You might think to yourself why is this? Why don't they just learn and master their products and services as well. The answer is simple, they just put it off and would rather just get by. Many also just don't think they need to role play and go the ectra mile. Most do not believe they could ever achieve the ratios I have mentioned so they would rather just be like most of the other 80% of sales people and be average. Sales people like you and I don't just settle. When I put you in my class, please note I am referring to the sales people that will actually apply this material and follow through. I know that many will not follow through, that is ok, you are still in a higher percentile than most for just reading the book and I expect your results will out way many of your sales associates. You may even become grcat, but the true great ones will be one of the top in the country.

Each of you have the choice of which one you can or will be. I challenge all of you to be great!

"The 5 P's
Proper Preparation Prevents Poor Performance"

"By being properly prepared you will prevent poor performance!"

"A sales person will go through more rejection in one day than

most people will face in an entire month and depending on the type of sales maybe even an entire year"

The 5 P's (Proper Preparation Prevents Poor Performance)

There are many important things to remember if you want to be a great sales person and if you want to be great, this is one of the most important things you will need to remember.

Proper Preparation Prevents Poor Performance!! This is so important that I will repeat it again. Proper Preparation Prevents Poor Performance!!

Think about it for a minute. Have you ever seen someone succeed in anything that wasn't properly prepared? I know that I in fact have never, ever seen someone succeed when they weren't properly prepared. In sports, there is a lot of practice. Even the baseball players who have mastered how to hit home runs must and do practice. That's why they continue to hit home runs consistently. This is true for any sport, Mike Tyson is one of the greatest and hardest punchers of all time, but do you think he ever went into a fight without prior proper preparation? That's my point exactly. When he won and he was on top of his game, he prepared properly and had a great performance. When he didn't prepare properly he had a poor performance which had nothing to do with his actual hitting power!

Proper Preparation Prevents Poor Performance!!

This is especially true in the professional industry. Do you think for a minute Johnny Cochran and the dream team could have won their impossible case had they all not been properly prepared? I'm not trying to create any controversy and not creating a political debate I'm just trying to prove a point. In that case, there were one set of professionals that were properly prepared who had all the odds stacked against them. On the other side stood a team that had everything going for them but since they were not properly prepared they lost. The truth or not is irrelevant! Proper Preparation will indeed Prevent Poor Performance. Poor Performance will indeed make you loose and fail in everything, sales, romance, business, sports and friendship.

If you want to succeed in everything, make sure you know the 5 P's! Proper Preparation Prevents Poor Performance!!

Some of you may still not be believers and might be telling yourselves that there have been times that two athletes that were both properly prepared there is always a looser. Well in reality, even when both are prepared one of them is usually better prepared. Also keep in mind when you have a team or individual that are facing opponents that are equally as prepared one side or another will loose, but at least they will still perform greatly!!

Chapter 11

The Greatest Sales Presentation in the World

For many years I have used what I believe is one of the greatest sales presentations in the world if not the greatest. This sales presentation is solely responsible for profits of hundreds of millions of dollars and hundreds of thousands if not millions of new clients around the world.

This sales presentation has proven itself and has been used through out the world and through out the country for many years. This very successful sales presentation is currently being used to this day by a few select companies that have had the privilege of working with the author. I have kept this powerful sales presentation secret for many years, and the only people who have ever seen it have been companies and individuals that have contracted me to consult for them individually or their companies. I figured how could I write the greatest sales book in the world and not include the greatest sales presentation in the world.

You might be asking yourself, this sales presentation does not sound very successful. It has only sold hundreds of millions of dollars in profit and only has a few million people as clients. There are many other companies that have sold billions of dollars in profits and have tens of millions of clients.

For those of you that have those thoughts, I would like to explain the reality of those thoughts. Most fortune 500 companies and companies that have billions of dollars of profits and millions of clients have been successful not using a sole sales presentation. Most of the companies I am referring to if not all of them were able to accomplish their sales with 50-100 separate sales presentations. Many of those companies review their sales material on an annual basis and many of them have many separate sales presentations they use regularly.

That is not to mention the hundreds of television commercials they run or the hundreds of separate radio commercials, direct mail, e-mail, faxes, web sites or even the many separate marketing companies they have hired to market them. Most of these successful companies generate a lot of sales solely on their commercials and name recognition generated by the hundreds of thousands of commercials they run monthly. I have consulted with several fortune 500 companies that include their commercials in their sales presentations to make it easier for their sales people to sell and easier for the consumers to buy.

That to me is not a very successful sales presentation, but a successful marketing strategy.

For many years my team and I would personally compete with many large companies known through out the country. Although the companies I represented and consulted for were unknown in many of the towns and cities I worked in and I was also an out of town stranger. I regularly competed and out sold very successful and very well known companies that were very well known using this sales presentation.

Why would someone buy from me instead of large well known companies?

The answer is very simple. I created and used a sales presentation that was superior to my well known competition. I also included in this presentation all of the things that the consumers would be thinking of and their questions and objections were overcome before they had a chance to ask or object. Most sales people with very large well known organizations try to avoid these topics from their consumers because they have nice cushy salaries and get paid to produce sales, not generate life time clients. They also do not fear their competition since they are large and well known, but if they knew how much business I took from them, they would fear me and have. Many have tried to recruit me so I would not compete with them and out sell them.

Although I have always been relatively small and relatively unknown. I have been highly recruited by many of the top executives of large companies when I roll into town. Although I could not compete with these companies on a financial or resource level, I can go into any of their markets and produce results, regardless of their presence.

I on the other hand get paid directly from my results and I have to not only produce results but compete against giants that have a lot more resources and finances well above what I have. They have the power to run television and radio commercials day and night and directly mail every consumer in town ten times. This is what I had to compete against and I overcame these challenges and succeeded.

Now, I will share with all of you the sales presentation that helped me take business from my giant wealthy competitors. I will also explain the sales presentation so you could understand.

I have adapted and customized this sales presentation in many different industries including but not limited to the mortgage industry, financial services, satellite dish, home alarm, insurance, real estate and health & fitness industries to mention a few. So if you have been looking for a proven sales presentation, I recommend you adapting this already proven and ready successful sales presentation that has already out produced many other companies around the country.

Let me first explain some of the sales presentation. The sales presentation is based on a 6 step sales arch. The sales arch is used in order to show sales people how the consumers buying emotions start at the bottom and is brought higher and higher top the top of the sales arch and then lowered to the close.

Once again, you should keep in mind that sales is a science and this is the sales formula that has been developed and mastered over the years.

A full sales presentation will follow, but right now I would like to let you know the 6 steps of a sale from the sales presentation.

But first let me give you some more examples of how powerful this sales presentation is. For the past few years I have consulted for many organizations in many different industries one of them being the mortgage industry as well as others. I'd like to give you some real figures to show you what the results have been using this sales presentation. Keep in mind that the sales presentation alone is not the sole reason for this success, but a part of it.

Mortgage Industry Results 2003

$365,400,000.00 Million in Annual gross sale volume

$30,450,000.00 Million in monthly gross volume of actual converted sales
$258,500,000.00 Million in actual funded loans

Keep in mind that these results are very respectable, but are low by some standards. Let me also add that these results were achieved from my consulting with only a few mortgage companies and these are the results of only 6 sales people!

Home Security Alarm Results 1 Year

405 new clients per month
4,862 new clients for the entire year

Once again, this may not sound that impressive to some, but it would be a lot more impressive if you knew these were the results of only 4 sales people!

Health & Fitness industry Results 1 Year

1,220 new monthly membership sales
14,640 new membership sales for an entire year

These are very impressive numbers especially since I didn't own the health & fitness centers, I just consulted with them and hired and trained a staff to generate those results. These results are also above and beyond any marketing campaigns that were being done by the health & fitness centers. Last but not least, these results were also reached with 6-8 sales people for the year.

Life Insurance (Mortgage Protection)

120 new monthly policies
1,440 new annual policies

This is HUGE! This was done as referrals to other companies mainly from business we already had. We used the exact same sales presentation. There were several insurance agents that did very well and we were their only source of business.

The list goes on and on, but I just wanted to give you some examples of some separate industries to prove the strength of this sales presentation. I also wanted to demonstrate that these were all primarily smaller companies in these industries. Although I have also consulted for many of the large giants in these industries, I have a soft spot for the smaller companies and with these types of results as I mentioned before, we out sold the giants and took as much business as we could handle, regardless of the presence of the better known giants in the industries.

In many of these instances we were actual brokers for the giants as well.

The presentation that follows is the exact presentation I have personally used for so many years in the mortgage industry and the exact same presentation I have trained so many mortgage professionals over the years. Keep in mind that this sales presentation can be customized for any service or product.

This particular sales presentation is also used in an in-home situation, meaning we went to their home.

Here are the six steps of the sales presentation;

Steps,
1. Greeting
2. Opening
3. Qualifying
4. Presentation
5. Pre-Close
6. Close

SALES PRESENTATION

Sales Arc

Qualifying	Presentation
Opening	Pre-Close
Greeting	Close

* Through out your entire presentation, you want to keep in mind that you just going through the motions to explain your services or products to your prospect in order to better meet their needs and answer their questions or concerns. Get away from the idea that you are selling them, you are just making sure that they understand you, your service or product and you need to be able to communicate it to them in such a way that there is nothing left to chance.

(Greeting)

Hello _____ how are you? I'm _____with XYZ Company (let them show you in if at their home or you show them to a sitting area)

(Talk to them about weather, their pets, house, anything to let them feel comfortable enough so they will lower their guard, since they are already skeptical about sales people and it's up to you to change that about yourself.)

So_____ can you believe this great weather were having? This is a great house, how long have you lived here? (Just some small talk, which should only take a few seconds and no more than a couple of minutes)

(Opening)

Is there somewhere we can sit and talk?

(Name) were you able to find the documents the (Appointment Setters Name), had mentioned to you? I need to review those items real quick.

(Make sure they get you all the documentation required and fill in the blanks on the 1003 with that info)

As you know we have reviewed your credit history and submitted your loan to our underwriter and we have already received your pre-approval, and can save you $_____. Per month which is $_____. Per year!!

I am not sure if you have been keeping up with the market but as you have probably noticed, interest rates have been at 40-year lows these past few months.

As you have also seen time and time again the only thing we know for sure is that the rates will surely go up again, it's just a question of when, and the rates have already begun to go up these past few weeks.

You're probable wondering why we came to your home?

The reason is pretty simple. Our research shows that even though the rates have been at all time lows there are a lot of homeowners that for what ever reason have not lowered their monthly payments on their mortgage and or debts.

We know it can be very confusing and frustrating and that is why we come out to visit our clients in the comfort of their own home. We also do this to provide you with additional customer service and we believe in going above and beyond most peoples expectations right from the beginning!

We would like all of our clients to feel comfortable and confident that they made the right decision.

The way we can accomplish our goal for our clients to feel confident that they made the right decision & at the right time is not only from us coming out but also by us educating our clients with their mortgage & other finances such as monthly debt. In this industry there are many different programs available and at times homeowners do not know which ones are out there or if they could qualify for the ones available, & that's how we build our clients confidence.

We also guarantee you the lowest possible rates & or closing costs with your mortgage, along with a guaranteed future refinance with our company at a minimal cost to you!

I will be showing you the program you have already been pre-approved for, & your monthly & yearly savings.

One of the best things that happen when we come to our client's home is the fact that we already have everything on paper.

We have you already pre-approved! Please keep that in mind through out our conversation that we already know we can get you these savings and we have taken the liberty to put it on paper and are ready to move forward!

We are not giving you different scenarios over the phone on what we may be able to do, we have already analyzed your credit history & reviewed your debt along with your employment income & have even submitted your loan to our underwriting department & they have already pre-approved you for these savings.

We also do this for word of mouth advertising, which not only generate repeat business but referrals as well. We are positive that once you have seen everything we are going to do for you, you will tell a friend, relative and that friend or relative will tell a friend and so on and so fourth.

If we treat you better than any other mortgage company you have already dealt with & we guarantee you the lowest possible rates & closing costs for your situation you wouldn't mind telling a neighbor, family member or friend about us would you? Of course not!

Later on when you ask yourself, what's the catch?

Now you know we are hoping that you tell a neighbor, family member or friend about us so we can help them as well!

There are a lot of companies out there that try to make a lot of money from a few individuals, we on the other hand by us going the extra mile and not taking advantage of our clients, that in itself cerate's a lot of word of mouth advertising for our company! We are looking to help more homeowner's instead of a select a few. That's the secret of our success!

(Qualifying)

(Remember the qualifying stage is your chance to gain ammo for later on in the sale, make your questions meaningful. Do not interrogate the person, just have a conversation "Dialogue" about the things they hope to gain from you (Us)! Do not interrupt them, unless they go on & on, get to know them a bit)

Let me ask you a few questions,

1. **Have you been thinking of lowering your monthly mortgage payments?**

2. **How long have you been thinking of lowering your monthly mortgage payments?**

3. **Have you spoken with any other mortgage lenders? If yes... how long ago?**

4. **What would you like to happen with your mortgage? (What kind of mortgage would you like?)**

5. **What exactly do you want in your new mortgage?**

6. **Now, in most cases we can consolidate some of your debt also to save you even more money, if we can roll some debt into your mortgage would you like that additional savings?**
   Great! So far it seems we can meet your needs, and save you money!

(Presentation)

(Here you are just using the information they gave you in the qualifying stage to show them what we can do for them, & how we are going to do it for them. Our goal here is to overwhelm them and over come the objections they mentioned to us in the qualifying stage! They have already told us what they want & don't want all we have to do here is meet their needs and assure them that no one will be able to do something better for them, & if they did find someone we will beat their rates & or closing costs so there really is nothing to loose with us!!
If their main interest was in lowering their rate, closing costs, consolidating some debt, focus on that and roll it into your presentation. Keep in mind that we may not be able to do exactly what they want & we are the professional's so we must explain why and let them know how we are going to do it. They do not know the mortgage business, we do. If they did they would have done what ever it is they want to do when the rates first went down over a year ago! Most times they just don't know they can't do something and that is why they have held on, because they think someone can do it & no one has explained that they can't, so they are amazed once they find out and end up doing what we can do for them.)

(Always use the assumptive with words 'you' and 'your' to refer to their mortgage we have for them. This makes them feel more of a part of our process along with using the assumptive sale. It also goes along with the main theme that we are simply going through the motions to finalize on their mortgage, & not selling it to them..)

Have you ever heard of us before? Well we are locally owned & operated. Were located at (Address). **(Begin to show them their savings sheet & or open your portfolio & or their file to show them their savings and begin the presentation)** let me show you the benefits and savings of your new mortgage.

(Show them the payment planer, their loan documents, certificate of guarantee, their savings, etc… and customize the presentation to their individual needs. This is where you will begin to use all of the weapons we have, that we have learned from the pre-qualifying questions! We must meet their needs!!! We must answer their questions before they've been asked, and we must overcome their objections once we know what they are.)

(Open their loan package & begin explaining the GFE, TIL, 1003, & show them their copy & get the authorization's needed.)

I am going to explain some of these documents. Most of these documents are required disclosures by law, which would be necessary for anyone.

The documents that will explain your loan are the 1003 application, good faith estimate (GFE), & the truth in lending. These documents right here will explain everything about your mortgage.

The 1003 application consists of 4 pages. This will have all of your personal information of who you are. It will also have your loan amount, interest rate, employment information, debts, income, previous address, & employment, bank account's assets, in general everything about you.

The good faith estimate also known as the GFE will have a break down of all costs associated with your loan. All hard costs, escrows, taxes & insurance. All costs are broken down for you in the good faith estimate. These are the hard costs of any mortgage. A hard cost is a cost that will be on any mortgage with any company. Those are fees that have to be there, that's why it's called a hard cost. The escrows are your taxes & insurance which you're already paying and will be rolled into your new mortgage. We'll be rolling all of the hard costs and escrows into the mortgage, there are a couple of hard costs associated with your loan that we are not allowed to roll into the loan.

1st is the appraisal fee and the other is the credit report fee.

The reason for that is many mortgage companies have relationships with certain appraisal companies as we do, & how would it look if we allow the appraisal fee to be rolled into the loan? Not good at all.

In some situations when that happens the underwriter will order a new appraisal with a different company & guess who foots that bill? You guessed it you do, & we better hope we can get the value we need with no trouble.

The other thing that we are not allowed to roll into the loan is the final tri-merge credit report.

We also have a relationship with the credit reporting agency, & this special tri-merge report usually clears up any old blemishes that might appear along with any duplicate accounts, & once again how would it look if we rolled that cost into the loan, not good. This is also a fee that we are charged the moment we order it.

I have seen the underwriter pull new reports with their agency & once again lets hope there are no surprises that they will question.

Keep in mind that this can help the report but does not guarantee there will not be any negative information on it.

Now the cost of the appraisal is $300 & the credit report fee is $65, most homeowners secure the appraisal & credit report with a check. Is that how you are going to secure the appraisal & report?

If Yes… all I need is a check for $365 & you can make it out to (Your Company Name). That's the only out of pocket expense there is, your pre-approval has the rest of the costs rolled into your loan. This is a one time investment of $365..00 that you'll get back next month! Everything else is has been rolled into your loan.

(If there is still any resistance because of the money get a check for the $65 credit report along with a $300 post dated check for the appraisal fee & we will roll it into the loan.)

That's the only out of pocket expense there is, your pre-approval has the rest of the costs rolled into your loan. This is a one time investment of $365..00 and that's all! Everything else is has been rolled into your loan.

Now the truth in lending a.k.a. the TIL, will show you the amount financed, and the annual percentage rate (APR). Let me cover something from this sheet, the APR shown is not the rate we have you at. This rate will always look higher than what it actually is, because we are rolling the closing costs into your loan. If you actually paid all of the closing costs up front the APR and your actual rate would match.

Please keep that in mind when you look at this it confuses everyone, the government requires us to disclose the APR to show the difference since the closing costs and escrows are rolled in.

All of these other documents are just disclosures on types of mortgages, state regulations, energy efficient homes, tax laws, & such. If you are bored later and want to fall asleep I recommend you read them, like I said these are given to any one who will be doing a mortgage. I will guide you through all of the pages that need your authorizations & date. You will see the highlighted sections.

(Have them sign their full name as it appears. Don't forget the date, you may want to make a couple of jokes about how many documents there are. It's like buying the house all over again. You may also want to remind them that this is not the closing and they will need to do this all over again at the actual closing.)

(Pre-close)

(To start the pre-close educate them with non threatening dialogue such as:)

Please keep in mind to not let anyone pull your credit history because it could change the rate & closing costs for the loan you have been pre-approved for. All loans are calculated the same way, loan to value (LTV) and debt to income (DTI), with these calculations they will now which program you would qualify for, the last thing that will determine the loan would be credit! So don't let anyone pull your credit.

Also keep in mind that your pre-approval & credit report will expire today, the reason for that is the market can change at any point and the rates can go up. Right now based on the information as we have it, we've already Pre-Approved you for these savings & once we've authorized these documents and disclosures we will be able to lock in your Pre-Approval today which means even if the rates go up tomorrow we have your new mortgage already locked so it won't matter!

The reason for the credit expiration is because, lets say all of a sudden 3 other companies pull your credit report, now the program we have you in might change because now your credit score dropped 10 to 15 points! Remember that for future reference, not to let anyone pull your credit report until we have finalized on your mortgage!

I don't want to worry you I just want you to be informed of the facts, in this case we'll be taking care of everything for you so we won't have to worry about that!

(Close)

(Again start a dialogue so they can sell themselves.)

"Great, I have copies of everything I've gone over with you that will stay here with you." *(Use the assumptive and begin taking their copies out and placing them beside them)*

Now we get to do the fun part, which is authorize all of these documents so we can finalize!

I have already highlighted the areas where we'll need initials, signatures & dates.

All we need to do now is authorize these documents and disclosures.

(Use the assumptive and place the pen in front of them on top of the documents that need to be authorized, assuming they will just begin authorizing all of the documents. Don't worry, if they have any questions or concerns they will ask at this point as they pick up the pen and begin authorizing)

If Questions... (This is not the closing all we are doing here is letting the underwriter know that we are ready to proceed and are authorizing the final approval!

(After all of the documents have been signed and we've collected checks)

Okay (Name) just so you understand what to expect, I'm going to be submitting this information to our processing department & you will be assigned a processor that will finalize from that moment forward. They will verify the information collected and set your file up, order the appraisal, title, get payoffs, etc...

It will still be at least a couple of weeks to a few weeks before we can close. As I mentioned the appraisal & title take a couple of weeks in itself.

The underwriter will also let us know if there is anything else we are missing. Just an FYI, it's their job to find something missing or request additional information, so at least know that we will most likely be asking for something else. It shouldn't be a big deal though!

(After they've signed all mortgage documents and disclosures, double check to make sure we have all of the information needed from them and that we have filled in the blanks on the 1003 application, along with credit explanations, etc.)

O.k. let me make sure we have everything here,
1 month of paycheck stubs
2 years of w'2's
3 months of bank statements
Statements on the accounts we are going to be paying off
Payment coupon on your 1st & 2nd mtg's
Copy of their note & deed of trust on their 1st & 2nd mtg's
O.k. it looks (Like we have everything, or we are missing?) can you (Make a not of the missing items and fax to me @) This is

something that we definitely need and this will slow the mortgage process if we don't get it. When do you think you'd be able to fax that to me?

(If there is anything missing make a note of it on the file, & have them write it down & make that there assignment for the next couple of days, if they need to get a new print out from their bank or a printout of their paycheck from their employer or what ever it is they are missing, except anything that deals with their 1ˢᵗ or 2ⁿᵈ mtg's!! Never have them call on their mortgage companies; it can cost us the loan)

(Any items they may be missing such as paycheck stubs, bank statements, etc. Just go on ahead and get what they do have and we will figure something out after we have everything else)

Well that takes care of that, definitely a few pages huh?

(Get 4 referrals, do not hesitate, just go right into it!!)

Okay (Customers Name) There is one last thing I need to mention. I can pay or lower your closing costs today, right now by $100 dollars! I have a voucher here that will allow me to pay $100 of your closing costs today, right now. We're only allowed to give you 1 voucher, which will consist of $25 per name and number on 4 names and numbers you refer to us today. We're only allowed to go up to 4, but then I'll be able to pay $100 dollars of your closing costs.

(Use the assumptive! Do not hesitate, pull the voucher out and place pen ready to write the names they give you once you've asked! Wait for the names and write them down on voucher!)

So, what's the first name and number?

(If there's any hesitation, let them know this could be a family member, friend, co-worker or neighbor)

Okay, great! I'll be giving you a copy of the voucher for your records, and I'll subtract the $100 right now from your closing costs.

That's it for right now. We will be locking in your loan today & we will be ordering your appraisal along with the title. The appraiser will be calling you to schedule a day & time for them to come by & appraise your home. If you come up with any questions just give me a call.

Common Objections

I just refinanced

We can still save you money, it looks like we not only will get you an even lower rate but it looks like we will be able to roll some of your debt into the loan and save you $_____ per month over what you are already paying! Your first year savings is$_____!

I have to talk to my bank

That's great, know when you go to your bank you can compare our rates to their's and see which situation will be best for you! Keep in mind that we will beat anyone's rates & or closing costs or both! In order for us to guarantee you these rates and closing costs I will still need the following information. (Do the sign off) but keep in mind that if your credit score drops it may change the current program we have for you.
You have nothing to loose, we are guarantying our program to be the best & are putting it in writing for you.

I want to shop around

(same answer as above)

If you can't get me 6% then it's not worth it for me.

We are currently saving you $_____ per month, & when the rates go down again we will be able to lower your rate even more & with minimal closing costs. The difference between the rate we currently have you at and the rate you want is only $___ per month less and we are saving you $_____ per month, the first year alone we'll save you! It definitely looks like this is in your best interest!

I already have a low interest rate

The rate I have you at is saving you $_____ per month! The first year we'll save you $___! Not to mention the fact that we will be refinancing you again in the near future at minimal cost to save you even more money! This is the best time to refinance and with us for those 2 reasons.

How long will this take?

It will only take a few minutes for me to show you how much we can save you.

How long before I get the money?

If we can work efficiently together I can have the money in your hands in 3 weeks. If you call any other mortgage company and they tell you that they can get it for you in less, they can't. Most national banks take at least 40 days, if you're lucky.

What kind of company are you?

We are a mortgage banker and broker. We are in the business of saving homeowners money by lowering their interest rate, and or consolidating their debt!

I have bad credit!

That's no problem we can help people in almost any situation.

(Bad credit, good credit, equity, or no equity, previous bankruptcy, even current bankruptcy)(Find out why they think they have bad credit, & get detailed Explanations) we have already reviewed your credit history & have you pre-approved! We have many different programs available and can help even those that have had credit problems in most cases! Let me just ask you a few questions and we will go from there.

Can you beat my low rate

Yes we can, we guarantee it! In most cases we've seen that we can lower the average homeowners current interest rate.

Is this a first mortgage?

Yes this will be a 1st mortgage.

I have already done a debt consolidation.

Well by our calculations we can still save you money.

I do not want to roll those things into my loan

A lot of people we talk with feel the exact same way at first, but once they find out the benefits of rolling in your monthly debt they realize it is in their best interest. We also need to in order to help the debt ratios for qualifying purposes.

I do not want to increase the balance on my mortgage

Most homeowner's say that at fist but to be totally honest with you, your balance is already that high. You already owe this money but in a worse way. You owe it at a higher interest rate which is compounded daily and at higher monthly payments. On top of that all of the interest that you pay on those high interest rates is not tax deductible, in our case we will be lowering the rates on those accounts more than half and at a fixed rate along with the fact that our rate is tax deductible this is definitely the best way to go.

I'm not interested.

There is no charge or obligation for the rate reduction analysis; I just have to ask a few questions
What is it that you're not interested in?
You're not interested in lowering your interest rate & saving money?
We can usually lower the average interest rate by 3% & save the average home owner 50% over their current monthly bills.
Wouldn't you like to lower your monthly bills?

30 year note

In order to get the kind of savings you want that is the best term for you, there is no pre payment penalty so if you wanted a shorter term all you have to do is add extra money to pay it off in the term you wanted.

I must speak with husband or wife :

No problem we hear that quite often, but your pre-approval has an expiration date so we need to at least secure the loan by taking care of the paperwork. This will give you a chance to speak with your (husband or wife).

I would like to think about it :

Sure go ahead and think about it, but your pre-approval expires today so we need to lock your loan so you are guaranteed to receive these savings and don't miss out.

Common Referral Objections

I don't know anyone to refer

Okay, (Customers Name) this doesn't have to be only a friend, it can be a family member, a co-worker, neighbor? In order for me

to pay $100 dollars of your closing costs, I just need 4 names and numbers of anyone you know. So, what's the first name!
(Use the assumptive and place pen on the voucher getting ready to write)

I don't know anyone looking to refinance

Oh, that's no problem! I don't need names of people looking to refinance, just names of people you know. That's all! So, what's the first name?
(Use the assumptive and place pen on the voucher getting ready to write)

I can't remember their numbers

Oh, no problem. Do you have your address book laying around anywhere? I can wait for you to look up.
-Or-
Okay, if you don't have an address book, maybe we can look them up in the phone book really quick, can you grab the phone book real quick?
(But get all of the first and last names first. Start with the names and numbers they do remember)

I just moved here from out of state and know no one
Oh, okay, well what states are the people you know?
-Or-
Okay, how about your co-workers at work? Or your neighbors? It doesn't have to be a family member or friend.

When using the assumptive (so which all I need are the authorizations on these documents!) You must also immediately follow up with using the assumptive by pulling the paperwork out and placing it in front of them with a pen pointing to the sections they need to authorize, at the same time! Those 2 assumptions have to be used in conjunction with each other every time!

These are some of the common objections that you are going to run across, and we can and have overcome them time and time again but you must use the rebuttals above no exceptions!

If you are serious about selling and are serious about increasing your income and sales you should customize the sales presentation to fit your services and products. I have personally used this sales presentation through out the country for the past 10 years. I have converted over 90% of all of the people I have met with over the past 5 years.

Also this is the exact same sales presentation I have trained all of my sales people and if you will look at some of the sales reports I have included you would also see that they close at very high ratios, higher than almost every other sales person in their industry.

Don't take my word for it, try it out for yourself!

The Assumptive

If there is anything you will remember from this book to increase your sales this should be it. This is the most important thing I have personally used for many years that has increased my sales dramatically and the sales of my staffs.

I have personally trained and worked with well over one thousand (1,000) telemarketers, lead generators and appointment setters. I was also the marketing director for a Two hundred billion dollar ($200,000,000,000.00) financial planning and insurance firm which I helped train many financial planners and insurance agents in selling. I have also recruited and trained a few hundred in home sales people for the health, satellite dish, and home security industries. And if that is not enough, I also recruited and trained several hundred in home mortgage directors, loan officers and real estate agents for many mortgage companies one of which is four hundred billion dollars ($400,000,000,000.00) strong.

All in all, I have personally trained hundreds if not thousands of sales people around the country. Sales people of all types of sales. In home sales, telephone sales, door to door sales, business to business. I have trained them all and what makes this story even more impressive is the fact that during these campaigns, all of the sales people I have trained that have worked directly under me or on my teams have all closed over seventy percent (70%) of the people they saw combined! Wow! This is very true and means that all of them put together converted at least seventy percent (70%) of the people they saw!

By anyone's standards those are unheard of numbers. They are almost unrealistic. Most sales managers and directors I meet with cannot comprehend these figures and regularly think the figures are inflated and exaggerated. I can assure you they are not. They are very real and for a fee, I will prove it to any person or company that retains my consulting services.

I don't tell you these ratios and all of the sales people I have personally trained over the years to impress you, I tell you to impress upon you the biggest most important thing that I train all sales people is the ASSUMPTIVE!

If you want more sales use the ASSUMPTIVE

This is truly the single most important thing I could teach you that you could implement that will get you immediate results. Don't just take my word for it, try it out for yourself. It really works.

If you see that I am being repetitive, it is because repetition is the mother of all success and this is that important. The assumptive is the most important thing to increase your sales!

The assumptive is the MOST IMPORTANT thing to INCREASE YOUR SALES!

The assumptive is so POWERFUL that it doesn't just work with sales. I have used the assumptive in many areas of my life. My business and personal life combined. I have used it meeting new people, I have used the assumptive to generate new business, new prospects, new contracts, new sales, referrals, everything. I have even used the assumptive to date women. I use it to get discounts at stores, to get things for free. I use the assumptive for everything I can. That is how powerful the assumptive is.

Assume the sale!

That is right, just assume the sale and more often than not, you will get it. Assume you will get referrals and more often than not, you will get them.

The way the assumption works is by saying and doing things during the presentation that assumes you will both be moving forward. After you have shook your head up and down enough times and had your prospect agree with you through out your presentation, and you have covered all of their questions, then the natural assumption is to close the sale. Why wouldn't you?

The assumption is also speaking with yes, yes questions. The first rule of thumb in sales is never to ask a question that might blow your sale. That would be a question such as, "Are you interested?" Well of course not? If you ask or give them an out, more often than not they will take the out. It is human nature, remember. We're all taught since we were children not to buy something or not to sign, or never do business on the first day and so on. So you should never as that question or any question like it. That would be the equivalent of asking someone "Would you like to buy this?" at the end of your presentation. That is a sales no, no.

Some of the outdated sales material have very good tools, but did not get into too much detail about some things. One thing is this very topic. I have heard many great sales people say things like, "you should always ask for the sale". That is a very powerful statement, and I would one hundred percent agree with that. How ever in many of those examples they do not explain how to ask for the sale. You should not ask for the sale in certain ways, like the examples I gave a moment ago. But you should indeed always ask for the sale, and if you want to have HUGE success in sales the way you should ask for it is by using the assumption.

Don't just ask but assume it. Assume the sale by sliding the sales agreement to them and putting the pen at the authorization line (Signature line) and saying something like "if you can authorize down at the bottom, the first to pages client just need your initials, then the ones after that will need your full signature". That is the assumption.

Assume they will do it.

Even in cases where someone is interested in purchasing your product, they may say no or not really or they want to think about it. They do this to be a better consumer. Or they may still have some unanswered questions. By using the assumption, those questions or objections will come out. Once they come out, the sale has just changed into a negotiation.

The sale just became a negotiation

Once you assume the sale there is one of two things that is going to happen. The prospect will either start signing the documents and ask questions as they sign or they will say something along the lines of, well how do I know this is what I will be getting, or how can I trust you, I've just met you, or I like everything you said but I want to think about it, or talk to my bank or other companies, etc, etc. This is also known as an objection and sales people are trained to overcome objections.

This is a very good sign, because now the sale just took a turn for the better. Now you know what is on their mind and they have just made a deal with you. In other words after your presentation if you asked the prospect to authorize some documents for you and you place the pen and documents which is using the assumptive in front of them, first of all their natural reflexes will get them to pick the pen up and also align the documents or contract for them to begin signing. That is the first thing that will typically happen regardless if they want to move forward or not. This is a good sign because it is still moving forward as if the two of you will be doing business together.

So if you have asked for the sale by using the assumptive and placed the closing documents or contract in front of the prospect and they ask a question which is an objection, now the sale has already been made and it has just turned into a negotiation.

For example; If you have used the assumptive as explained in the previous paragraph and the client says, well this or that. It does not really matter what they say. If you have asked for the sale and they ask or request something, the prospect is effectively saying "Okay I will buy your products or services and sign your contract, but first answer me this. Or first convince me again why I should sign". Get it? The sale has been made and the client wants you to reassure them why they should do business with you or why they should buy your products or services.

Objections are good

I love hearing objections, because as explained above once I hear an objection, the sale was made and it is now my turn to accept their negotiation and answer (Overcome) their questions then they will sign the documents I have placed in front of them. They are the ones that started the negotiations, and as a sales person I know what I can or cannot do as far as my product is concerned so I will know exactly how to accept or counter offer the prospect. But the sale was made.

The sale starts with the objections

I think that most sales begin when the objections start. If that were not the case then anyone could be taught how to memorize a simple presentation and everyone would get the same exact results. I actually believe and practice this philosophy, but it is not quite that easy. Yes anyone can memorize a sales presentation, but most importantly, they must memorize their rebuttals, because in reality, the sale starts with the objections and if you are not prepared to field all of those objections or negotiations you will loose the sale no matter how good the presentation is.

The presentation is to explain the product or service one hundred percent so that you and the prospect can focus on how you will move forward. The presentation is for the product the rebuttals are for the prospect.

So master your rebuttals. If you do not have any, create some. With every product or service, there are really only about 10-15 objections that will come up over and over again. This is true for almost any product or service. If you are not sure what they are for your product or service, ask your sales manager if they have any material on their rebuttals or in the training manual. If they do not, don't be alarmed I will teach you how to create them from scratch. If you are wondering why I first said go to your sales manager first instead of us just creating them from scratch?

It is because we should not attempt to reinvent the wheel when ever it is not necessary. There are most likely sales people that were with your organization way before you got there. There are also most likely many sales people that have had tremendous success with your organization that sell the same products and services you will be. Typically they have already learned what the rebuttals are and have already been through the trial and error you will most likely go through so why try to reinvent the wheel when you could take a short cut and save yourself weeks, months or even years.

If they do not have any material, then you may want to approach the top 1-2-3 sales people in your organization and pick each of their brains. I can almost guarantee you that the top producer has already created some material of their own that they use. Even if they have not put it on paper, I can almost guarantee you they use a particular formula and say the exact same things. They also will know what the top 10-15 rebuttals are from their prospects. Find out what they are.

If that does not work refer to the rebuttals that work chapter in this book. There you will learn for yourself how to find out what the top 10-15 common objections to your sale and also the top 10-15 rebuttals to overcome them.

Remember the 5 P's Proper Preparation Prevents Poor Performance! The assumptive works hand in hand with the rebuttals and overcoming their objections. If you use the assumptive which you should if you would like to increase your sales, you better be prepared and have all of the objections and rebuttals memorized. Using the assumptive alone is not enough. It will take both, the assumptive is the best and strongest way to close a sale. The assumptive will spark the client to search for an objection to begin their negotiations, so you must be prepared. If you use the assumptive alone your results will increase, but no where near as much as if you combine the assumptive with the rebuttals.

This is also the single most important thing I have taught all of the sales people I have trained over the years. I'm talking about all of them,

The Close

The Close! This is the area that most sales people and sales trainers around the world focus on. Most people think that the close is the most important part of a sale. I would agree to a certain extent. By now you've probably seen and read enough of this book to know that in order to have great success in sales, there are many things that have to take place, not just one thing. You must have a product you believe in, a great sales presentation, a great set of rebuttals, a great assumptive and then a great close in order to reach your goals and objectives. The close alone will not do it.

So for those of you that thumbed through the other chapters and sections looking for the all mighty close, first go back and read all of the chapters because the close alone will not get you the results you are looking for.

That being said, lets get started. The close is a very large part of successful selling. There is nothing I seen worse than a sales person doing a great sales presentation and overcoming objections to not ask for the sale! That is one of the worst things a sales person could do! Essentially asking for the sale is the close. I also like to consider the close as the assumptive. By assuming the sale you are asking for it. In other words when I place a pen and sales agreement in front of my prospect, that is the same thing as asking for the sale, I'm just not coming out and asking "are you interested" which is something I would never do.

Keep in mind that asking for the sale, does not mean ask for the sale. Let me explain, as my previous example showed, you would never, ever ask a prospect "Are you interested"? That would be the worst thing you could do. They are expecting that and have been trained for many years on how to answer that and overcome that to the point that you will loose the sale. That is also a yes no question which is one of the worst things a sales person could do. You should always ask yes, yes questions. We've covered this in the previous chapters, but I know repetition is the mother of all success, so I'll also repeat important things.

Getting back to the close, assuming the generation of the lead, appointment, sales presentation and overcoming the objections went as it was supposed to, then the close is the most important part of the sale.

The Waiver Form or Cancellation Form

I also used other closing tools as well to increase sales. I developed a waiver form (Cancellation Form) that helped increase sales through out the country by 20%! That is huge! Imagine converting or closing 20% more sales by just using one tool. Not generating any new additional business but just using or saying one or two paragraphs extra. In other words, just meeting with and presenting with the same amount of prospects you would get 20% more sales!

The way I came up with this idea was when I was on the road running sales and marketing promotions through out the country. I used to have to rent automobiles when I'd get into town. I remember one of the auto rental places scared the heck out of me and for the first time ever I almost got the extra insurance. He said to look over the policy waiver and sign it stating I did not want it. When I read it, it stated that I could possibly be liable for damages to the vehicle if I did not have insurance and such. It was a very powerful paragraph that literally made me think of getting it, although I already had my own insurance and was also using a gold card that would automatically cover me in case anything happened.

Wow! What a powerful sales technique. I consider myself to be smarter than the average person and I almost bought into it. I figured that this company most likely sold more insurance policies than anyone else for their rental cars by using such a form. I was sure of it. I also figured that by doing this, this auto rental store had a whole new profit branch. I mean they are in the business of renting automobiles, that's how they make their money. But by being so successful in the insurance side of it, they probably double their income without having to double their automobile rentals or increase their clientele. That's when I figured I could do the same with myself and my sales staffs.

I then came up with the cancellation form and I included it into all of the sales presentations. I first began using it on my own so I could perfect it and then roll it out with my sales staffs.

I saw an immediate increase in my conversion ratios. I was already one of the best closers I new and the #1 closer in my entire organization. At the time I had already closed about 70-80% of everyone I had met with for over 3 consecutive years. If you've ever sold anything, you'll know that to do that for 1 week is tough, to do it for even one month is unlikely but to do it for over 3 consecutive years in a row is unthinkable. Let me assure you that it is absolutely true. Never the less, my conversion ratios went from about 70-80% to 95-100%.

After perfecting the cancellation form, I closed 100% of everyone I saw for several months in a row. It was amazing. I then rolled it out with the entire sales staff in the entire country and sales jumped by over 20%!

It was a brilliant idea if I do say so myself. I'll be including an example of the cancellation and waiver forms. I've used this form in three separate industries and it has had the same results in all of them. I'll include the forms for the fitness industry sand also the mortgage industry to show you. I'll also include the rebuttal or presentation of the form. Keep in mind that once we presented the form, we used all of the wrong terminology that a great sales person would normally not use to get a sale. In this case we wanted to do the exact opposite and not sign the form so we used the wrong verbiage so they would sub consciously not want to do it and it would get us back in the door to figure out how we could proceed and get the sale.

Also we only presented this form as a last resort. Once the prospect has told us no and when we tried to overcome all of their objections and failed.

Also please note that the way the form looked and needs to look is also a huge factor with the results you will get. It must look official and be on a 2 piece carbonless form to add to the official effect mof the form.

The client would keep a copy of their form for their records and we would keep the original. Think about it? Can you see the effect? Just following the system and them keeping a copy and us keeping the original?

Here is an example of what the mortgage waiver form looks like.

MORTGAGE APPROVAL WAIVER FORM

Due to the rapid and continuous change in the bond market which directly affect mortgage interest rates, your mortgage pre-approval had a 24 hour guarantee. If you wish NOT TO ACCEPT your mortgage pre-approval which is reserved for you with an interest rate of _____%, monthly savings of $_____ and the first year savings of $_____, you must sign this mortgage approval waiver form which will cancel and void your pre-approval.

I understand that by signing this WAIVER FORM, I am giving up this mortgage approval and I forfeit the rate, closing costs and all the savings. I also understand that I may never receive another opportunity at this rate with these savings.

_____   _____
Waiver's Signature   Date

_____   _____
Telephone #   Date

_____   _____
Mortgage Directors Signature   Date

Waiver's reason(s) for not accepting the Approval:_____
_____
_____
_____
_____

Can you see how powerful the waiver form is. The form alone is not what makes it so powerful, the form along with the negative key words and the presentation are what make is so affective.

Did you catch the negative words?
Cancellation! Waiver Form! NOT TO ACCEPT! Must Sign! Void! They are giving up!

Those are very negative and powerful words. Keep in mind those words are their to get the sale by making sure they do not want to sign the waiver form. Get it?

In other words, by making the waiver form sound and seem negative, they will second guess their decision of not wanting to buy and now they will most likely not want to sign the waiver form which gives us another chance at being the good guys which we are and try to figure out how we can help them.

Also notice how we get their name and number. This is for our future marketing so we can try and save the few that actually go through with it and sing the waiver form.

Here is the way the waiver form is presented. Once again keep in mind we would normally never ever use these words when actually trying to get a sale. Once we're using this we're already lost the sale and now are trying to save the sale without having to badger the prospect.

Waiver Form Presentation

Okay (Prospect Name), I need you to read this form very carefully and sign the bottom. This form is to help protect you and us. In the past there have been times when we've met with a client and for what ever reason they did not move forward, and all of a sudden the market changes and rates go up dramatically. We've had clients calling us asking for the same rate and program.

Although we've told them the rate no longer exists and is not available on the market anymore it has created some problems. Clients have actually said they were not aware they would not be able to get the rate in the future and had they known they would have indeed moved forward. This is why we have this form, so you can be completely aware of the fact that this rate and program may not be available to you even tomorrow or next week. We want to make sure we've done everything in our power to try and educate our clients so they can make the correct decision!

So what do you think? Can you see how this simple yet affective form could help increase your sales?

This is a powerful form and presentation, but you must be careful. I have seen on several occasions' sales people that tried to rely, solely on the waiver form to get sales, then you actually see their sales drop although even with a lower ratio it is higher than what their ratios were before so it throws everything off. A sales person could be converting 70-80% using everything, but if relying solely on the waiver form they may be converting only 60-70% which by their standards would still be good, but by my standards not optimum!

Chapter 12

Telemarketing Campaigns that work

Telemarketing

This is my favorite sales and marketing topic! This is where I rule! I consider myself the king or god in many areas of sales and marketing, but many around the country know me or would consider me the king or god of telemarketing.

I don't personally know anyone that has started as many call centers as I have through out the country. I also don't personally know anyone who has consulted for as many industries as I have and have created as many telemarketing campaigns as I have.

I have personally created telemarketing campaigns and call centers for the health and fitness industry, satellite industry (Satellite Dishes), home and business security (Alarm Systems), Real Estate, Mortgage, Insurance, Financial planning, Financial Services, Mortgage Protection and others to mention a few.

Telemarketing is a $700,000,000,000. Billion Dollar Industry

The Telemarketing industry is one of the largest industries in the country. Currently the telemarketing in the United States alone generates over $700 Billion dollars annually. That's right over $700 Billion with a B in case you were wondering if that was a mistake.

As I write this there also over 7,000,000 Million telemarketing employees working in over 70,000 call centers in the United States!

Those figures are very impressive and speak for themselves!

The telemarketing industry is HUGE!!

As you have probable heard though the telemarketing industry has come under attack. The attack is coming from new state and federal law regulating telemarketing companies and individuals alike. I think most of these laws are bios and do not stand for one of our main rights in our country which is the 1st amendment of freedom of speech.

We live in a society of free enterprise which is one of the greatest privileges we have as Americans. Unfortunately the government has recently set their sights at the very needed telemarketing industry there by trying to eliminate a free enterprise society.

Do not get me wrong, I know there are many bad and unprofessional telemarketing companies out there and the government should absolutely go after those companies and close them down. The entire industry should not suffer for the acts of only a few. That would be the equivalent of the government regulating the automobile industry because of a few used car shysters that have taken advantage of consumers.

So to all of you that might have participated in placing yourself on a no call list of some sort, I would strongly recommend that you not participate in these unfair government practices to attempt to eliminate an American industry that generates $700 Billion American dollars to our country and employs over 7,000,000 (Million) Americans!

That being said, let me introduce you to one of the most affective ways to generate new business. This is a direct contact industry that will save you the most valuable asset you have, time. With a good telemarketing or cold calling campaign, you are assured one thing. More leads, appointments and more business. That is a guarantee.

Most business people and consumers alike tend to have a negative connotation to the telemarketing industry. Most consumers and business people alike rarely believe the statistics on how large the telemarketing industry really is. Anyone with simple common sense would agree that any industry generating this kind of volume and employing so many people could not possible be as bad as it has been unfairly portrayed.

Be prepared for rejection

The reason for this unfair portrayal is for many reasons some even stemming from the people that have worked in the industry. Over the years I have heard many thousands of people that at one point or another have cold called either because they had to, had a part time job, or as a teenager was the only job they could get.

So for many people this was an unpleasant thing they had to do in their life. Also because of the unfair portrayal of the industry and the type of work, most people speak negatively when discussing with others. Most people think that if they say they are a telemarketer that others would look down upon them!

Telemarketing is probably the one industry that has the most amount of rejection of all other industries put together. It is no surprise why most people that have done it before have a negative feeling towards it.

Imagine getting rejected more in one day than the average person gets in an entire year. Or getting rejected more in on month than the average person gets in an entire year. That is right, telemarketing and cold calling will in fact get you the most rejection than you have ever had before with anything else.

Do not be alarmed. Because with the most rejection will come the most results. A great example is Babe Ruth, he has the most home runs of any other batter, yet he has been stricken out more than any other batter as well.

Michael Jordan once said he only succeeds because he fails. Michael Jordan one of the best basketball players of all time has also missed more shots than almost all other players as well.

These kinds of results are similar to telemarketing. Well not really similar, with telemarketing you will have a lot more rejection and failure. So be prepared. You should also be exited, because if you stick with it. If you don't let it get to you, you will also achieve a higher level of success than you have ever reached before.

So it is a shame when people pass judgment or speak negatively towards telemarketers. It is also sad to see telemarketers ashamed of what they do simple because of the negative press it has received over the years.

What a shame to be ashamed of such a noble duty. This is hard work; even dish washers take pride in their work and get credit by others for being a hard worker. Let me tell you! Telemarketers are some of the hardest workers I have ever met, in more ways than one.

Telemarketers are also looked down upon as being low paid employees. Well like any industry there are many different levels of pay. Let me tell you this, in most industries there aren't many entry level positions that you need no education and not many skills to start and literally have the opportunity to earn $50,000-$60,000 and even $100,000 plus per year in a very short period of time. Think about it? What other industry other than sales which telemarketing is definitely a form of sales, can you start with no prior training, experience or education and have the opportunity to earn over $100,000 per year? None that I can think of!

One of my very good friends who I have had the pleasure to work with and also help him with his telemarketing skills works from his home telemarketing and earns over $150,000 per year and he loves it. He is a family man who takes his two children to school each and every day along with picking them up daily as well. He drives a very expensive classic sports car, has a boat, motorcycle and nice home.

The best part of it as he tells me is all of his free time to do what ever he likes. He lives this lifestyle and could absolutely live a lot better life, but he is very content with his $150,000 per year working from his home. He loves the fact that he can earn this kind of living and have this kind of lifestyle and he only works about 15 hours per week!

He is a professional telemarketer!

Almost all of his work is done over the phones cold calling strangers.

He loves that fact, yet he still does not describe himself as a telemarketer or cold caller. He is proud of the fact though. He will disclose it when people ask how he generates his business, and then he is more than happy to bring it up. Especially since most people praise him when they find out and are shocked he earns so much.

This is only one of many stories. I have many, especially since I too earn my money through telemarketing. I wouldn't say only telemarketing, but mainly telemarketing. To this day I still cold call since it is one of the most effective ways I know of generating new business. I also run a call center that generates most of my lead and appointments for me.

I still telemarket or cold call on my larger clients and also to establish new consulting contracts for myself.

Telemarketing is what I would consider direct contact marketing. You are contacting a prospect directly.

Telemarketing in itself is the most effective way to reach new business. There is no other way to reach as many prospects in the same amount of time. Even if you went door to door, or business to business you would not be able to reach as many prospects.

There is also not really any other way of guaranteed results. That is for sure. By telemarketing and cold calling you are guaranteed to generate new leads, business, appointments which in turn will result in more sales.

Telemarketing and cold calling are a numbers game

Telemarketing and cold calling is absolutely a numbers game. So be prepared for a lot of rejection, because the numbers or odds in telemarketing are stacked against you! Depending on what it is exactly that you are cold calling for, how good or not you are, and also the scripts. You will most likely speak with about 20 people before getting one yes. That has been the average I have noticed with almost any industry. But that has been with any industry with any telemarketer experienced or not.

With an experienced telemarketer and proven scripts, I have seen this number decrease dramatically. I have seen an experienced telemarketer with proven scripts generate one application or appointment per ever four to five people spoken with.

Those numbers are very consistent with experienced telemarketers and proven scripts. A telemarketer of mine once generated applications and appointments out of every four to five people spoken with for over a year. I am sure it lasted well over a year, I only tracked this particular telemarketer for a year.

No experience telemarketing and no proven script does not matter!

One thing I have also learned is the fact that regardless of being experienced or not. Having a proven script or not is also irrelevant. It would be foolish to say it does not help. Of course an experienced telemarketer and proven scripts would absolutely help! But not having either does not really matter.

I have trained thousands of telemarketers over the years that have never picked up a phone before. There is really only one thing that someone must have, self assurance. They must be or feel confident and not take things personal. It is not personal. The person on the other end does not know you. When someone is rude over the phone to you, it is not because of you or what you do. They do not know you, so how could it possible be you? They would react this way with anyone. It could be you, me or anyone.

The only criteria you must have is perseverance and you must not take it personally.

You must have thick skin. If you do not. Do not worry, but stick with it and I can assure you, you will develop it very shortly!! I promise you.

Let me give you an example. If you do not have any experience telemarketing or cold calling. It really does not matter. As I have said before, it is a numbers game.

Telemarketing and cold calling is really one of the only industries if not the only one where you can get immediate results regardless of experience. Which other industry do you think you could get immediate results that same minute, hour, shift?

If you began selling automobiles, you will most likely not be able to sell an aout the first day. If you sold furniture or did financial planning, or was even an attorney over night. It is very unlikely that you would get results the first day you started. It is actually very unlikely that you would even get any results the first week or even first month.

With telemarketing, if you make your calls and learn a script, you will most likely get results the very first hour of calling.

I have tested my theory and has is know a fact. If you had no proven list or telemarketing skills, if you just picked up a phone book. It does not matter if it is the yellow or white pages. It does not matter if you are calling businesses or consumers.

If you picked up the phone right now and began calling every business or consumer listed in the phone books from A to Z and if all your script said is "Will you meet with me tomorrow at 6pm?" You would in fact get an appointment. That is a fact. You would eventually get an appointment. The question is not whether you would get an appointment, because you would. The question is how many people you would have to speak with before getting the appointment.

In that example let's say you might have to speak with fifty people in order to get one to agree.

Let me take this example a step further. Let's say that you now didn't just call people and ask for an appointment. Now you are calling and saying, "Hi, I am calling you regarding your home loan -or- Hi, I am calling regarding your homeowners insurance –or- Hi, I am calling regarding the security of your home –or- Hi, I am calling regarding your finances, will you meet with me tomorrow at 6pm?"

Now your results might increase a little bit. Now you might only need to speak with twenty people to get an appointment.

And let us say that you would like to increase your results even more. Now you change your strategy again and now when you call people, you say "Hi, I am calling regarding your home loan, and it looks like I can save you quite a bit of money on your home payments, would you meet with me tomorrow at 6pm? Your results would continue to get even better.

You continue changing your strategy, over and over again. You do this to increase your results.

So now, you change your strategy yet again and now when you call people, you use the assumptive and say this "Hi, I am calling regarding your home loan and it looks like I can save you quite a bit of money over what you are currently paying on your home loan. I will be in your area tomorrow and can meet with you at 6pm, or would 7pm work better for you?"

Your results would increase even more.

By doing this, you will get guaranteed results. By continuing to change your strategy over and over again and using what works and getting rid of what does not, your successes would continue to rise!

Try it and see for yourself.

Ask yes, yes questions

Whenever selling in general you should always ask yes-yes questions, but that is especially true when telemarketing and cold calling. Yes, yes questions are questions that the only answer has to be yes. Or even if the answer is not yes, it will should not be a no. There are times when you can ask a question which the answer could be no, but it is not a no to purchase or buy anything. In other words, lets say you are telemarketing and trying to set an appointment, you would not ask "Would you like to meet?" or "Do you have time to meet?"

Those would be yes / no questions. Get it? The prospect could say no and then it's almost over. Now if you try to talk them into it, you become the annoying telemarketer and it makes it easy for them to be rude and or hang up on you!

The prospects are expecting and waiting for you to slip up with a silly question like that, but no more. You will now have the skills not to fall into that trap.

If you want to succeed and increase your results and level of success you will need to start asking yes-yes questions. Questions that you already know what the answer is going to be and you are prepared to answer or overcome any objections.

Here is how you would like to ask something like that. You also want to remember the assumptive, as I have mentioned before. One of the most important things in selling is the assumptive and the assumptive can and should be used in every aspect of selling, lead generation and appointment setting. So if you wanted to meet with a prospect you should ask like this, "So (Prospects Name) I'll be in your area tomorrow and I can stop by and meet with you, so would morning or afternoon work better for you?"

See this would be an example of a yes-yes question. You are not asking if they want to meet, yes-no. You are asking would morning or afternoon would work better for them?   There is one or two answers that you can expect from this type of question. You can expect a Mornings or afternoons answer, or the second answer will be a neither. In that case, then you would over come it with pre-scripted rebuttals. Something along the lines of, "okay (Prospects Name) so it sounds like evenings would probable work better for you, so how's 6:30pm sound?"

That way you are taking their own answer and using it. No one like's to be known as a liar, so when they answered that mornings or afternoons would not work, in my eyes that means evenings would work better. They are not expecting that, so you are that closer to setting the appointment with them. So a neither is not bad, because you will have pre-scripted rebuttals to overcome that without having to be the pesty telemarketer.

See if they say neither, you still win and you should expect that response. So if they say neither, you could say, use the rebuttal we just covered.

The Greatest Lead Generation Script in the world

Considering the fact that I have opened and created from scratch at least 50 inbound and outbound call centers around the country and have consulted and created many inbound and outbound telemarketing rooms for many organizations in several different industries, I am considered by many including myself to be a telemarketing expert. There have been many different industries I have created successful new telemarketing campaigns to generate new leads for many companies in very different industries and organizations.

After many years of successful telemarketing campaigns around the country, there is one telemarketing script that I could consider to be the greatest telemarketing script in the world! It is the best in an industry with regulations that are very strict. This amazing telemarketing script is in the mortgage industry and has generated astonishing and amazing results.

The greatest telemarketing script in the world generates not only new leads and business, but also collects information. This amazing telemarketing script is not only a script to generate new business and leads but it is also a fact finder. It is also designed to collect information including very personal and private information in one of the most difficult financial applications ever designed.

For many years I have tracked my results and the results of those individuals and organizations I have trained and consulted for.

How One Telemarketer Generated $879,840,000.00 MILLION in one year!

One telemarketer alone with no previous background in finance or sales was able to generate and average 390 new mortgage applications per month which is a yearly volume of 4,680 new mortgage applications in one year alone using this incredible telemarketing script.

Considering that the company I was consulting for had an average new mortgage amount of $188,000 per new mortgage.

That one telemarketer alone generated a gross monthly mortgage application volume of $73,320,000.00 MILLION per month!!

That one telemarketer alone generated $879,840,000.00 MILLION in new mortgage applications for the year!!! That one telemarketer alone with no previous mortgage, finance, or sales experience generated almost $1 BILLION dollars in new mortgage applications for one year!!!!

Although these numbers do not sound realistic, let me assure you they are very real. I have seen a team of five full time telemarketers in the past that for other organizations that were not able to generate the volume of one of my top producers. All of my telemarkers have always out produced other telemarketers for other organizations. That was one of my selling tools in the past. When I would approach an organization part of my sales strategy was to help the organization generate more business than they can generate using their techniques alone, using my proven marketing and sales strategies to generate more business with less overhead than they are already spending.

Think about it?

How many business owners do you know would like to earn more business and money spending less than they are already spending? Of course everyone would like this. You'd be a fool not to.

The way I would achieve this was by re training or hiring new telemarketers and get them to use these proven scripts and combine the scripts with proven telemarketing and sales techniques.

Let me go into more detail of the information needed on this mortgage pre-qualification application.

The information needed in order to be able to turn in a mortgage pre-qualification application was:

- Full names of all people on their current mortgage
- Social security numbers of all parties on the mortgage
- Employers
- Yearly income
- How long with their employers
- Mortgage Balance
- Appraised Value
- Purchase Price
- Year Purchased
- Monthly mortgage payment
- Amount of their taxes & Insurance
- Interest rate
- Adjustable or not
- If they have a 2nd mortgage or not
- ….If yes, then the same information on 2nd mortgage
- Previous bankruptcy, yes or no
- Previous foreclosure yes or no
- Any late payments on anything
- Any mortgage late payments yes or no
- ….if yes, how many? 30's, 60's 90's?
- Additional information relating to the application and their home

Wow!

That is a lot of information required to get for these applications. As if that was not enough, the typical mortgage company that I consulted for well unknown. This one telemarketer I am referring to was not calling previous clients. He was not calling for a well known mortgage company. In fact he was calling for an unknown mortgage company that was only about 2 years old.

You might be asking your self, "how is this possible?"

How can only one telemarketer generate such a HUGE volume of business by himself?

How can he get so much personal information, especially when the prospects don't know him or his company?

I would like to point one other thing out. He was not able to turn in all applications, there was some criteria that all his applications also had to have. They all had to have an interest rate at a certain rate and type before he or anyone else could turn it in?

In reality, he generated a lot more volume than what he is even given credit for. The reason for that was because we new the mortgage interest rates where at a certain level, and we also knew that if someone was at a rate lower than what we could offer them then it would be irrelevant. Not only that, but it would make us look bad that we went through all of the work and not be able to help them, so that might affect their view of us in the future.

We didn't just waste those prospects, we asked them other questions in order for us to cross sell them something else. We used those applications to refer them to financial planners, or insurance agents to see if we could lower their monthly homeowners policies. We also asked if they would like to lower their monthly credit card debt, or of they wanted to purchase investment properties. We did not believe in wasting these applications of prospects that are willing to work with us and give us necessary information that would enable us to use as leverage to generate more business in other areas or also get us in front of other industries where we could generate referral business.

Another thing I would like to point out, for the skeptics. I have heard many people mention that we called certain people with certain types of mortgages in order to generate these kinds of results. Although I have presorted lists in the past and depending on the type of company, prospect and industry I am working in, I still may sort a list, but in the mortgage industry, the only thing we sorted was businesses and renters. Although we had a renters campaign to help renters purchase a home, the only criteria we had for our mortgage lists was that they had a mortgage. I know the law of averages, and I know we can get results by calling everyone. We called people with good credit, bad credit, high mortgage balances, low mortgage balances, rich, poor, all neighborhoods, all areas. We called everyone.

Some of you might be thinking why would we call everyone. Well, because I have seen many people with good credit still end up in bad mortgages and we could help them. I have also seen way too many people that had good credit, but have fallen on bad times and know need help and vise versa. I have also seen many people with bad credit who have worked very hard to fix their credit and can know unknowingly qualify for a better program for them. So it is very affective to call everyone. The law of averages will take over. As I have said before, sales and marketing is a numbers game.

Some people have also told me that is not the best strategy because we would be wasting our time talking with the people we can't help. Or the ones that already have low rates, etc, etc. We'll I know this game pretty well and I also know those are usually the ones that will hang up on us. They know they just refinanced last month and may have the most competitive rate on the market. I know they won't talk with us, because even if we could help them, they will hang up. I know the ones that can't qualify, have already had many other companies tell them that and they also might hang up or not waste their time or ours.

I know the numbers and know there are a certain percentage of people that will hang up, not give us an application, not give social security numbers, etc, etc.

I encourage you to also look at all of the information we generated from these mortgage applications.

How many separate industries can you think of that can use this information? I'll list a few that I have not only worked with but also used this same information to generate new business and sales in these other organizations:

- Mortgage
- Real Estate
- Home owners insurance
- Mortgage protection (Life Insurance)
- Financial planning
- Credit repair
- Home improvement

Those are just a few separate industries that I have also worked with the greatest telemarketing script in the world, but it is not only limited to those industries. I have seen many companies also cross reference this information with other companies such as:

- Carpet cleaning
- Home security
- Satellite dish
- Home repair
- Deck companies
- Landscaping

Those are also just a few companies that can be cross referenced with the exact same information from the information gathered from the mortgage applications.

Of course you would have to use a separate script to adjust to the different products which we are not going to cover here. But I'm sure you can figure that out after looking at the material in this book.

Now the moment you have all been reading about and waiting for, let me introduce you to the greatest telemarketing script in the world. I am also going to be including some other versions of other great scripts and also examples of other very successful telemarketing scripts for other industries.

Some of you might think the greatest telemarketing scripts in the world might be very complicated, let me warn you that is not true. The greatest telemarketing scripts in the world that I have created and also have worked with are the exact opposite of that, which is a secret formula that I think helps with its results.

It is a misconception that a good telemarketing script has to be long and difficult. In actuality it is the exact opposite.

Okay, so with out further to do, it is my pleasure to introduce all of you to;

The Greatest Telemarketing Scripts in the world!
Mortgage, Real Estate Buying or Selling, Financial Planning (Services), and Survey Scripts

* TELEMARKETING PRE-QUAL PHONE SCRIPT *
MORTGAGE INDUSTRY

HELLO CAN I SPEAK WITH (customers name),
HI (customers name) THIS IS (your name) WITH (COMPANIES NAME), I'M CALLING IN REGARDS TO YOUR MORTGAGE THAT WAS WITH (mortgage co. name), IT LOOKS LIKE WE MAY BE ABLE TO SAVE YOU QUITE A BIT OF MONEY OVER WHAT YOU'RE CURRENTLY PAYING ON YOUR MORTGAGE!

ALL I NEED TO DO IS JUST VERIFY SOME BASIC INFORMATION FROM YOU OVER THE PHONE AND THEN WE'LL KNOW WHICH PROGRAM WILL SAVE YOU THE MOST MONEY.

(GO RIGHT INTO THE APPLICATION WITHOUT ANY HESITATION!!)

(Name) YOUR FULL NAME IS_____, AND I HAVE YOUR ADDRESS DOWN AS _____ WHAT CITY IS THAT IN?
(customers name) IS THERE GOING TO BE ANYONE ELSE ON THIS APPLICATION?
     IF YES…. (GET THE OTHER PERSONS FULL INFORMATION)
     IF NO….(CONTINUE! TAKE THE APP!)
(FILL INTO APPLICATION)
WHAT IS THE CURRENT VALUE ON YOUR HOME?
WHAT IS THE CURRENT INTEREST RATE ON YOUR MORTGAGE? IS THAT FIXED?
WHAT IS THE BALANCE ON YOUR MORTGAGE?
WHAT IS YOUR MORTGAGE PAYMENT? DOES THAT INCLUDE TAXES & INSURANCE?
WHAT WAS THE PURCHASE PRICE ON YOUR HOME? HOW LONG AGO WAS THAT?
WHAT TYPE OF MORTGAGE DO YOU HAVE? (FHA, CONVENTIONAL, VA)
DO YOU HAVE A SECOND MORTGAGE?
IF YES… WHAT IS THE BALANCE, INTEREST RATE, PAYMENT, DATE YOU GOT THE SECOND MORTGAGE.

(COMPLETE THE ENTIRE APPLICATION. CONTINUE TO ASK ALL QUESTION ON THE APPLICATION, DO NOT HESITATE)

* TELEMARKETING PRE-QUAL PHONE SCRIPT *
MORTGAGE INDUSTRY

HELLO CAN I SPEAK WITH (customers name),
HI (customers name) THIS IS (your name) WITH (COMPANY NAME), I'M CALLING IN REGARDS TO YOUR MORTGAGE THAT WAS WITH (mortgage co. name), IT LOOKS LIKE WE MAY BE ABLE TO SAVE YOU QUITE A BIT OF MONEY OVER WHAT YOU'RE CURRENTLY PAYING ON YOUR MORTGAGE!

(GO RIGHT INTO THE APPLICATION WITHOUT ANY HESITATION!!)

(Name) YOUR FULL NAME IS_____, AND I HAVE YOUR ADDRESS DOWN AS _____ WHAT CITY IS THAT IN?
(customers name) IS THERE GOING TO BE ANYONE ELSE ON THIS APPLICATION?

      IF YES.... (GET THE OTHER PERSONS FULL INFORMATION)
      IF NO....(CONTINUE! TAKE THE APP!)

(FILL INTO APPLICATION)
WHAT IS THE CURRENT VALUE ON YOUR HOME?
WHAT IS THE CURRENT INTEREST RATE ON YOUR MORTGAGE? IS THAT FIXED?
WHAT IS THE BALANCE ON YOUR MORTGAGE?
WHAT IS YOUR MORTGAGE PAYMENT? DOES THAT INCLUDE TAXES & INSURANCE?
WHAT WAS THE PURCHASE PRICE ON YOUR HOME? HOW LONG AGO WAS THAT?
WHAT TYPE OF MORTGAGE DO YOU HAVE? (FHA, CONVENTIONAL, VA)
DO YOU HAVE A SECOND MORTGAGE?
      IF YES... WHAT IS THE BALANCE, INTEREST RATE, PAYMENT, DATE YOU GOT THE SECOND MORTGAGE.

(COMPLETE THE ENTIRE APPLICATION. CONTINUE TO ASK ALL QUESTION ON THE APPLICATION, DO NOT HESITATE)

The script that follows is a script I used in the mortgage and real estate industries to create alliances with mortgage and real estate companies. The way it worked was the mortgage company or broker would either call themselves to generate a Comparable Market Analysis (CMA) lead that he would give to a real estate agent. The real estate agent would benefit because they would get leads and increase their business and the mortgage person would benefit because they would capture the mortgage on some of the leads that went through and the real estate agent would also refer the mortgage professional additional business.

* TELEMARKETING SETTING APPOINTMENT WITH A REAL ESTATE AGENT *
REAL ESTATE INDUSTRY

Can I speak with the person who handles the Home Buyers?

Hi (Name), this is (Your Name) with A & M Consulting, we have a buyer that's ready to start looking for a home and we need to refer them to a real estate agent. Are you the person I should be speaking with?

> If No... Okay, who should I be speaking with?
> > When is (He, She) going to be available for me to speak with?

> If Yes... Continue!

Great!
(Name) We'd like to drop his file and approval letter over to you for you to take a look at and to speak with you a little more about it!
(DON'T HESITATE! SET APPOINMTENT!)
Our director's going to be in your area tomorrow, so would morning or afternoon work better for you?

Ok (Name) if you can please jot down the time. You'll be meeting with (Directors Name) at (Time) tomorrow!

Thanks for your time! Bye!

Oliver P. Maldonado

This is the script used to actually generate the Comparable Market Analysis (CMA) from actual homeowners. It worked extremely well. Each of my phone reps would generate about 4-6 per hour. We would then use the script before this one to set appointments with and meet real estate agents. I then had them sign agreements with me stating that I would be generating them CMA leads and in return they would also match what I sent them or match a certain ratio of what I sent them. This was a very effective way to double the real estate and mortgage volume.

Real Estate Buying or Selling Script (CMA)

(Name), would you like to know what the value of your home is worth? We can provide you with a free property value analysis so you can know what your home is worth and how much it has gone up in value!

Would you like a complimentary property analysis?

Okay, I have your address as? Your name as…

(Don't hesitate, get the information)

Although I have created hundreds of mortgage scripts over the years for separate mortgage campaigns and to maximize what ever is going on in the markets and communities, those two scripts by far are the greatest I have ever implemented and used and they work in any economy. I have used those exact scripts when the rates are low, high and when the economy was good and bad. They have worked consistently for many years. Those are the exact same scripts used by the telemarketer I used as an example who generated almost $1 BILLION dollars in one year of mortgage applications! So believe me they work.

160

I was considering including many of the mortgage applications I have used in the past, but I did not want to confuse you or have you attempt to create other types of scripts based on the other examples. I'm showing you the greatest scripts in the world. I have had people in the past hang out in front of my offices trying to get my telemarketers to sell them my scripts. Now I am including them in this book. I can assure you these scripts work!

I would like to mention that these scripts alone don't just work. It is a combination of things that make the scripts the success that they are. Just using a successful script alone is not enough. You have to recruit the right kind of people, which is also what helps generate the type of results I have given. Proper training on how to read the script, is also required, but most importantly the script is meant to be used with rebuttals. I can assure you that this is not some magical script where all you do is read it and you too will be able to generate almost $ 1 billion dollars in one year using it. No, no, that is not the case and will most likely not happen. But I can assure you the best results you have ever achieved is you use the script consistently along with the rebuttals. And you must use the rebuttals with every one.

Before I get into the rebuttals, I will include some other very successful scripts I have used for other organizations in different industries. I would also consider these other scripts as being the best in those industries. I have also used these scripts to out produce the expectations and results those industries were used to.

My next example of scripts are also very great scripts, but they target a different audience. The next couple of examples are for the financial services industry. I had the privilege to be contracted to create a telemarketing campaign for a very large financial services giant. The organization was over 165 years old and had a net worth of over $200 BILLION dollars. That was impressive when I accepted the offer, but what was even more impressive to me, was the fact that about 95% of their business was through referrals and word of mouth. Now that is what I call very impressive and unheard of for me.

So these next few scripts are from this industry and worked very well. I created these scripts to cater to the way this organization did business and through referrals which was obviously successful with this organization. You'll also notice that the scripts are a little soft, but it worked for the target audience we targeted and called upon. They were very successful scripts and campaigns that worked very well.

FINANCIAL SERVICES TELEMARKETING SCRIPT

HELLO _____,

THIS IS (YOUR NAME) WITH THE (YOUR COMPANY) LOCATED AT (YOUR ADDRESS). I AM CALLING TO EXTEND TO YOU A TOTALLY FREE FINANCIAL ANALYSIS WITH ONE OF OUR TOP AGENTS, (AGENTS NAME). IT CAN BE ON ANYTHING YOU LIKE; FINANCIAL PLANNING, RETIREMENT PLANNING, DISABILITY INSURANCE, COLLEGE FUNDING, ESTATE PLANNING, RETIREMENT, OR BUSINESS IN GENERAL. PLEASE CALL ME AT 000-000-0000, EXTENSION 000 AND I WILL SCHEDULE AN APPOINTMENT AT YOUR CONVINIENCE.

THANK YOU,

FINANCIAL SERVICES TELEMARKETING SCRIPT

HELLO _____,

THIS IS (name) WITH THE (YOUR COMPANY), WE ARE CONDUCTING OVER THE PHONE SURVEYS EXTEND TO YOU A TOTALLY FREE FINANCIAL ANALYSIS WITH ONE OF OUR TOP AGENTS, (AGENTS NAME). IT CAN BE ON ANYTHING YOU LIKE; RETIREMENT PLANNING, DISABILITY INSURANCE,

COLLEGE FUNDING, ESTATE PLANNING, RETIREMENT, OR BUSINESS IN GENERAL. PLEASE CALL ME AT 000-000-0000, EXTENSION 000 AND I WILL SCHEDULE AN APPOINTMENT AT YOUR CONVINIENCE.

THANK YOU,

PHONE SCRIPT (SURVEY-APPOINTMENT SETTING)

HELLO _____,

THIS IS (name) WITH THE (COMPANY NAME), WE ARE CONDUCTING OVER THE PHONE SURVEYS & BY PARTICIPATING IN OUR SURVEY WE WILL GIVE YOU A TOTALLY FREE GUIDE, THERE ARE OVER 10 YOU CAN CHOOSE FROM!
THE SURVEY CONSISTS OF JUST 5 QUESTIONS, LETS BEGIN!

1. HAVE YOU OR YOUR SPOUSE EVER THOUGHT OF PROTECTING YOUR MORTGAGE IN THE EVENT THAT SOMETHING WE'RE TO HAPPEN TO YOU OR YOUR SPOUSE? _____

2. IS YOUR MORTGAGE CURRENTLY PROTECTED? _____
3. HAVE YOU OR YOUR SPOUSE EVER THOUGHT OF YOUR RETIREMENT PLANNING? _____
4. HAVE YOU OR YOUR SPOUSE EVER THOUGHT OF ANY OF THE FOLLOWING, COLLEGE FUNDING,ESTATE PLANNING, TAX PLANNING, DISABILITY, OR BUSINESS IN GENERAL? _____

5. DO YOU OR YOUR SPOUSE FEEL YOU COULD BENEFIT FROM A TOTALLY FREE FINANCIAL ANALYSIS WHICH WILL OUTLINE ALL OF YOUR FINANCIAL NEEDS, GOALS? _____ —

THANK YOU FOR PARTICIPATING IN OUR SURVEY! FOR YOUR PARTICIPATION WE WOULD LIKE TO GIVE YOU A FREE GUIDE OF YOUR CHOICE, WE HAVE (list the guides), SO WHICH ONE WOULD YOU LIKE TO RECEIVE?

(name) FOR YOUR PARTICIPATION IN OUR SURVEY YOU WILL ALSO RECEIVE A FREE FINANCIAL ANALYSIS. YOUR FREE FINANCIAL ANALYSIS WILL CONSIST OF A FREE

CONSULTATION IN THE COMFORT OF YOUR HOME SO YOU CAN SEE WHAT YOUR FINANIAL GOALS, NEEDS & WANTS ARE & HOW TO GET THERE! YOUR CONSULTATION ONLY TAKES ABOUT 15 MINUTES, SO WOULD MORNING OR AFTERNOON WORK BEST FOR YOU?

THANK YOU,

The next example I am including was for the same organization who part of their financial planning was based on life insurance policies. Life insurance is also very profitable. We targeted homeowners based on mortgage protection in the event something happened to their loved ones, their mortgage would be taken care of. It's a brilliant concept that did help a lot of families and also helped the organization increase their life insurance policy sales, not to mention the fact that they were able to generate a lot of financial planning business as well.

PHONE SCRIPT (CALLING DIRECT MAIL)

HELLO CAN I SPEAK WITH (names)?

HI (names) THIS IS (your name) WITH (COMPANY NAME) FOLLOWING UP ON THE INFORMATION I SENT YOU LAST WEEK REGARDING THE PROTECTION FROM YOUR MORTGAGE WITH (lenders name) IN THE AMOUNT OF ($ laon amount), DO YOU KNOW WHICH MORTGAGE I AM TALKING ABOUT?

(name) IS THAT (lenders name) MORTGAGE BEING PROTECTED?

DO YOU KNOW ABOUT MORTGAGE PROTECTION?

If no ... (CONTINUE)

O.K. MORTGAGE FREE HOME PROTECTION GUARANTEES YOUR FAMILY A MORTGAGE FREE HOME IN THE EVENT THAT SOMETHING WERE TO HAPPEN TO YOU OR YOUR SPOUSE BEFORE THE MORTGAGE IS PAID OFF.

DO YOU KNOW IF YOUR MORTGAGE IS PROTECTED?

If yes … (ask) HOW MUCH PROTECTION IS THAT? HOW MUCH ARE YOU PAYING FOR THAT PROTECTION? WHAT KIND OF PROTECTION IS THAT?

I JUST NEED TO VERIFY SOME INFORMATION FROM YOU & MAKE SURE THAT YOU HAVE THE RIGHT TYPE OF PROTECTION. (verify information)

If no … (CONTINUE)

(name) I JUST NEED TO VERIFY SOME INFORMATION FROM YOU OVER THE PHONE SO I CAN DO SOME RESEARCH & SEE WHAT STEPS WE WOULD NEED TO TAKE.

(begin verifying information)

O.K. THAT'S ALL OF THE INFORMATION I NEED RIGHT NOW. (name) DO YOU HAVE A PEN HANDY? I NEED TO GIVE YOU SOME HOMEWORK. I NEED YOU TO GATHER THE FOLLOWING ITEMS I WILL NEED TO REVIEW …(list items). (name) WHEN DO YOU THINK YOU'LL BE ABLE TO GATHER ALL OF THOSE ITEMS?

O.K. GREAT! I WILL BE IN YOUR AREA ON (date) SO I CAN COME BY TO REVIEW THAT INFORMATION FROM YOU, IT SHOULD ONLY TAKE ABOUT 15 MINUTES,
(SET APPOINTMENT! DO NOT HESITATE!)
SO WOULD MORNING OR AFTERNOON WORK BEST FOR YOU?

As I mentioned before as with any successful script, there must be rebuttals used in conjunction with the scripts, so I will also include the rebuttals to these scripts. Use them with the scripts and you should expect some good results, use any scripts with out any rebuttals and you should expect very poor results, or poor results compared to my standards.

The Greatest Rebuttals in the World

REBUTTALS

CAN YOU JUST MAIL ME THE GUIDE?

I'M SORRY WE CAN'T, THE FREE GUIDES ARE DELIVERED TO YOU BY OUR DIRECTORS WHO WILL ALSO CONDUCT YOUR FREE FINANCIAL ANALYSIS WHICH NEEDS TO BE DONE IN PERSON. PLEASE KEEP IN MIND THAT YOUR FREE FINANCIAL ANALYSIS WILL ONLY TAKE ABOUT 15 MINUTES & WE ARE NOT TRYING TO SELL YOU ANYTHING, SO WOULD MORNING OR AFTERNOON WORK BEST FOR YOU?

WHY DOES SOMEONE HAVE TO COME TO MY HOME?

SINCE WE WORK WITH A LOT OF CLIENTS & SOME OF THEM PAY US A LOT OF MONEY FOR OUR SERVICES WE WOULDN'T WANT TO CREATE A CONFLICT SINCE YOU WILL BE GETTING A FREE FINANCIAL ANALYSIS, SO WOULD MORNING OR AFTERNOON WORK BEST FOR YOU?

WE HAVE A LOT OF REQUESTS FROM CLIENTS WANTING US TO COME OUT TO THEIR HOME SO OUR DIRECTORS SPEND A LOT OF TIME OUT OF THE OFFICE VISITING WITH CLIENTS, SO WOULD MORNING OR AFTERNOON WORK BEST FOR YOU?

WHAT'S THE CATCH?

THERE IS NO CATCH, WE PROVIDE THIS SERVICE TO YOU AS A CUSTOMER SERVICE. WE FIGURE THAT IF WE COULD HELP YOU & SHOW YOU HOW TO REACH YOUR FINANCIAL NEEDS YOU MAY CHOOSE US FOR YOUR FINANCIAL NEEDS & EVEN REFER YOUR FAMILY & FRIENDS TO US. SINCE YOU WILL RECEIVE A FREE FINANCIAL ANALYSIS THEY WILL AS WELL, SO WOULD MORNING OR AFTERNOON WORK BEST FOR YOU?

The Greatest Rebuttals in the World

Although there is something that must be said for a well written telemarketing script, I have learned over time that great scripts alone will not generate the best results possible. There is no such thing as a magical script and the ones that produce magical results is achieved using well prepared rebuttals.

For instance, the example I gave you before on one of my telemarketers that generated almost $1 billion dollars of mortgage applications in a single year also achieved those results by using the rebuttals more than anyone I have ever worked with. Although I manage and strongly encourage everyone to use their rebuttals all the time, he used his rebuttals religiously on every person he spoke with, and as a result, he generated more mortgage applications than anyone person I have ever worked with consistently.

Every industry has rebuttals. There is about ten things that will always come up with every industry along with products and services. These ten common objections are inevitable. They are the things that are most common to your products and services that people always think of. What you need to do is find out what yours are. If you are not sure, I would recommend going to the top producers in your company and ask them what they think are the most common objections they have to overcome and what it is they say to overcome them. There will be your rebuttals.

If you are a new business owner you can also do the same with your competitors. Believe me, a great sales man is always glad to help. There are also conventions and shows for every industry that cover these topics. You shouldn't try and reinvent the wheel when someone has already done the necessary research available that you can follow and learn from.

Don't reinvent the wheel

I'd like to give you an example I heard many years ago. I read in one of the many sales and marketing books I read about two of the largest fast food chains in the world. They are both hamburger fast food chains. I won't mention their names here, but I'm sure you could figure out who I am referring to. Anyways, I read that one of the fast food restaurants spend about twenty million dollars per year researching areas to build new restaurants, while the other only spend about five hundred thousand per year. I was blown away by that. There is such a huge discrepancy on that number which in today's dollars fifty million per year. Anyways the strategy of the other very successful fast food restaurant is to open a new restaurant within 5 miles of the other. How genius is that? That is a brilliant idea, all they have to do is let their competitors spend all of the time, energy, research and money and they will have the exact same benefit of their competitor's efforts!

It's absolutely brilliant!

If you'll notice it is true. You will always see both of the restaurants very close within a few miles of the other. At first some thought that was not the best idea because, some people may only like the other restaurant and they may corner the market. But who ever thought up that brilliant plan must have known the law of averages and know there will be an equal amount of people that would prefer their hamburgers as well as the other restaurant. They knew they also had a proven formula with their hamburgers and restaurants and that's all they needed.

So I encourage all of you to follow the same example and use the experience your competitors have already discovered and use what they use.

I'm sure the other fast food chain could have invested the same amount of money and energy researching areas to develop new restaurants, but they would have had invest twenty million per year to find out the same exact information, not to mention the trial and error they would have to go through to do it.

So use your resources and don't try to reinvent the wheel unless you have to.

Since I have used the example of the greatest telemarketing script in the world, it only makes sense to use the exact rebuttals that also had an impact in making it the greatest telemarketing script in the world.

The rebuttals I will show as examples are the exact same rebuttals that helped the telemarketer I used as an example earlier. These rebuttals were developed especially to be used in conjunction with the greatest telemarketing script in the world.

I cannot mention enough how very important rebuttals are in order to have a successful telemarketing campaign along with the consistency of using the rebuttals.

STANDARD RE-BUTAL SHEET

ANY QUESTION YOU DON'T KNOW THE ANSWER TO

I DON'T KNOW THE ANSWER TO THAT. LET ME JUST GET SOME INFORMATION FROM YOU REAL QUICK THEN I WILL HAVE A PROGRAM DIRECTOR CALL YOU BACK WITH THAT INFORMATION, I HAVE YOUR ADDRESS DOWN AS... (DO NOT HESITATE TAKE THE APP)

I JUST REFINANCED

GREAT! WHAT KIND OF RATE DID YOU GET? HOW LONG AGO WAS THAT?
HAVE YOU EVER THOUGHT OF CONSOLIDATING SOME DEBT? WE CAN TYPICALLY LOWER YOUR MONTHLY COSTS BY UP TO $600 DOLLARS! WE CAN USUALLY CUT YOUR MONTHLY DEBT INTO HALF! THAT'S A 50% SAVINGS TO YOU!
THAT'S GREAT, BUT KEEP IN MIND THAT INTEREST RATES ARE AT AN ALL TIME LOW, & WE HAVE A LOT OF OTHER PROGRAMS AVAILABLE THAT MIGHT SUITE YOUR NEEDS JUST AS WELL!

WHY DO I HAVE TO GIVE MY SOCIAL SECURITY NUMBER OVER THE PHONE?

BECAUSE IN ORDER FOR US TO VERIFY YOUR CREDIT

HISTORY, AND HAVE AN ACCURATE ACCOUNT ON WHICH
PROGRAM WILL SUITE YOUR NEEDS THE BEST WE WILL
NEED THIS INFORMATION. AND WHAT WAS YOUR SOCIAL
SECURITY NUMBER?

WHAT IS YOUR INTEREST RATE?

IT'S BASED ON A COUPLE OF THINGS. ONE IS YOUR PREVIOUS
CREDIT & THE OTHER IS YOUR MORTGAGE HISTORY. LET ME
JUST GET SOME INFORMATION FROM YOU AND A DIRECTOR
WILL GET BACK WITH YOU.
I DON'T KNOW THAT INFORMATION, I JUST TAKE THE
APPLICATION OVER THE PHON. LET ME JUST ASK YOU A FEW
QUESTIONS, AND ONE OF OUR PROGRAM DIRECTORS WILL
CALL YOU BACK WITH THAT INFORMATION.

I HAVE TO TALK TO MY BANK

THAT'S GREAT, KNOW WHEN YOU GO TO YOUR BANK YOU
CAN COMPARE OUR RATES TO THEIR'S AND SEE WHICH
SITUATION WILL BE BEST FOR YOU! ALL I NEED TO DO IS ASK
YOU A FEW QUESTIONS AND WE WILL BE ABLE TO GIVE YOU
A RATE!(GET THE APP)
WE DO HAVE SOME OF THE LOWEST RATES CURRENTLY ON
THE MARKET, & IN MOST CASES WE HAVE OTHER PROGRAMS
THAT LOCAL BANKS DO NOT HAVE. WE CAN DO WHAT
OTHERS CAN'T IN MOST SITUATIONS THEY WILL ONLY TELL
YOU WHAT THEY HAVE & NOT WHAT YOU NEED! KEEP THAT
IN MIND.

I WANT TO SHOP AROUND
(SAME ANSWER AS ABOVE)

IF YOU CAN'T GET ME 6% THEN I AM NOT TALKING WITH YOU?

ALL OF OUR PROGRAMS ARE BASED ON A COUPLE OF THINGS
YOUR PAST CREDIT HISTORY AND THE AMOUNT OF EQUITY
YOU HAVE. LET ME JUST ASK YOU SOME QUICK QUESTIONS
AND WE'LL LET YOU KNOW.
WE MAY OR MAY NOT BE ABLE TO GET YOU THAT, LET ME

JUST ASK YOU SOME QUICK QUESTIONS THEN WE'LL LET YOU KNOW!
DON'T YOU THINK IT'S IN YOUR BEST INTEREST TO SEE IF WE COULD GET YOU THAT RATE?

I ALREADY HAVE A LOW INTEREST RATE

THAT'S GREAT, BUT IN MOST CASES WE HAVE SEEN THAT WE CAN STILL DROP YOUR CURRENT RATE & CONSOLIDATE YOUR DEBT. ON AVERAGE WE CAN LOWER YOUR RATE BY 2-3% & SAVE YOU UP TO $600 DOLLARS PER MONTH!

HOLD ON, I FIRST HAVE TO TALK WITH MY (HUSBAND, WIFE)

THAT'S FINE WHAT I WILL DO IN THE MEANTIME IS JUST GET SOME INFORMATION FROM YOU SO THAT I CAN SEE HOW I CAN HELP YOU.(IF NO) O.K. LET ME GIVE YOU MY # AND EXT. AND AFTER YOU SPEAK WITH (HIM, HER) AND HAVE ANY QUESTIONS THEN CALL ME BACK AND I WILL BE ABLE TO HELP YOU OUT.

HOW LONG WILL THIS TAKE?

IT WILL ONLY TAKE A COUPLE OF MINUTES FOR ME TO SOME INFORMATION FROM YOU, THEN THE PROGRAM DIRECTOR WILL CALL YOU BACK AND LET YOU KNOW EXACTLY WHAT WE CAN DO FOR YOU.

HOW LONG BEFORE I GET THE MONEY?

IF WE CAN WORK EFFICIENTLY TOGETHER I CAN HAVE THE MONEY IN YOUR HANDS IN 3 WEEKS. IF YOU CALL ANY OTHER MORTGAGE COMPANY AND THEY TELL YOU THAT THEY CAN GET IT FOR YOU IN LESS, THEY CAN'T. MOST NATIONAL BANKS TAKE AT LEAST 30 DAYS, IF YOU'RE LUCKY.

WHAT KIND OF COMPANY ARE YOU?

WE ARE A MORTGAGE BANKER. WE ARE IN THE BUSINESS OF SAVING HOMEOWNERS MONEY BY LOWERING THEIR INTEREST RATE, AND OR CONSOLIDATING THEIR DEBT!

WE ARE ALSO ON THE WORLD WIDE WEB, AFTER I GET SOME INFORMATION FROM YOU WHY DON'T YOU CHECK US OUT.

I HAVE BAD CREDIT!

THAT'S NO PROBLEM WE CAN HELP PEOPLE IN ALMOST ANY SITUATION.
(BAD CREDIT, GOOD CREDIT, EQUITY, OR NO EQUITY, PREVIOUS BANKCRUPTCY, EVEN CURRENT BANKCRUPTCY)
WE HAVE MANY DIFFERENT PROGRAMS AVAILABLE AND CAN HELP EVEN THOSE THAT HAVE HAD CREDIT PROBLEMS IN MOST CASES! LET ME JUST ASK YOU A FEW QUESTIONS AND WE WILL GO FROM THERE.

CAN YOU BEAT MY LOW RATE

IN MOST CASES WE'VE SEEN THAT WE CAN LOWER THE AVERAGE HOMEOWNERS CURRENT INTEREST RATE, by 1-3%.

HOW DID YOU GET MY NUMBER?

WE HAVE A LIST OF NAMES THAT WE GOT FROM A DATABASE.

IS THIS LIKE A LOAN?

WE HAVE ABOUT 15 DIFFERENT PROGRAMS, I AM NOT TO SURE ON THE DETAILS, BUT OUR PROGRAM DIRECTOR CAN CALL YOU BACK IN ABOUT TWENTY MINUTES WITH ALL OF THAT INFORMATION. I JUST TAKE THE APPLICATION OVER THE PHONE.

IS THIS A FIRST MORTGAGE?

WE HAVE OVER FIFTEEN DIFFERENT PROGRAMS, I AM NOT SURE ON THE DETAILS BUT I KNOW THAT THERE ARE FIRST AND SECOND MORTGAGES THAT WE HAVE AVAILABLE, OUR PROGRAM DIRECTOR WILL HAVE ALL OF THE DETAILS WHEN THEY CALL YOU BACK.

I HAVE ALREADY DONE A DEBT CONSOLIDATION.

THAT'S GREAT, WE MAY BE ABLE TO SAVE YOU MONEY ON YOUR CURRENT FIRST MORTGAGE.
GREAT, HAVE YOU BEEN THINKING ABOUT DOING ANY HOME IMPROVEMENTS?

I HAVE LOW INTEREST RATES ON MY CREDIT CARDS.

WE HAVE SEEN THAT MOST OF THE PEOPLE WE TALK TO
AVERAGE BETWEEN 18 TO 22% ON THEIR INTEREST RATES,
IF YOU HAVE LOW INTEREST RATES IT IS MOST LIKELY
TEMPORARY AND WILL MOST LIKELY GO UP.
THE BOTTOM LINE IS SAVINGS ON THE AVERAGE WE CAN
SAVE YOU ABOUT 50% ON YOUR CURRENT MONTHLY BILLS,
THIS WILL NOT COST YOU ANYTHING AND THERE IS NO
OBLIGATION, WOULDN'T YOU LIKE TO SAVE UP TO 50% OVER
YOUR CURRENT PAYMENTS.

I'M NOT INTERESTED.

THERE IS NO CHARGE OR OBLIGATION FOR THE RATE
REDUCTION ANALYSIS, I JUST HAVE TO ASK A FEW
QUESTIONS
WHAT IS IT THAT YOU'RE NOT INTERESTED IN?
YOU'RE NOT INTERESTED IN LOWERING YOUR INTEREST
RATE & SAVING MONEY?
WE CAN USUALLY LOWER THE AVERAGE INTEREST RATE BY
2% & SAVE THE AVERAGE HOME OWNER 50% OVER THEIR
CURRENT MONTHLY BILLS. WOULDN'T YOU LIKE TO LOWER
YOUR MONTHLY BILLS?

Okay, I think you can get the idea of what a successful script should be like. All you have to do is make a script sound like the examples I have given along with similar rebuttals and you will also have some successful scripts in your hands. After that, the only thing that will help you get good results is to start calling and continue calling until you get the results you are looking for.

I can assure you that you too can generate as many leads as you want. Put a little bit of time and effort into your scripts and rebuttals and I guarantee you could reach what ever number of new leads or business you would like.

How can you get as much new business as you'd like?

As I have said a lot through out this book, it's a numbers game, so if you wanted 1 new lead. Then call until you get 1 new lead. If you want 50 new leads, all you have to do is call use your script and rebuttals and don't stop calling until you have gained 50 new leads. If you want 100 new leads. Break it down into how long it took you to get 50 new leads and split it up into how ever many days it will take for you to reach it. I can guarantee if you don't stop trying and calling you will hit your number. It might take 1-2-3 or even 10 days to reach your goals, but so long as you don't quit, I guarantee you will hit what ever it is you'd like.

Keep in mind, just because you set one number and reach it, does not mean your calling is over. You should set a continuous weekly and monthly goal that will be ongoing to supplement your new leads and business.

The Greatest Appointment Setting Script in the World

Although we have covered some great script and rebuttal ideas, new leads are worthless unless you get in front of them. You could have a million new leads, but if you don't figure out an effective way to get in front of them, you will not be able sell anything to the 1 million new leads, which would make them worthless.

So just like you need to include the use of rebuttals with your lead generation scripts, you will also need to implement effective appointment setting scripts and rebuttals in order to maximize your lead generation campaign. Telemarketing campaigns are not a 1 call process. It is a step by step approach to help develop a relationship and confidence from a complete stranger, and that goes both ways. The stranger who became a prospect and who may also become a client needs to build confidence that although he or she does not know you or your company, that the few times they have spoken on the phone with you, they are beginning to trust you which will lead to them doing business with you. But as they build trust in you, you will also start building trust in them that they are serious and are not wasting your time. So it is important to follow these necessary steps in generating first new leads, then new prospects, then new appointments that will lead to new clients.

I have shown you the greatest telemarketing script in the world, now I'm going to show you the greatest appointment setting script in the world.

Let me first give you some background on this appointment setting script. As with all of my material in this book, I have used it for many years and it has proven itself over the years through out the country and very successfully I might add. I'm only including the very successful things I have done created and used successfully over the years. Although I have had many other scripts and ideas that we're not always as successful, you will have the benefit of the trials and errors I have already gone through and can use the very best from scratch. I'm a big advocate of not reinventing the wheel if you do not need to.

Just like the lead generation scripts and rebuttals, the assumptive as I have said through out this book is one of the most important tools sales people can use. It is one of the most effective ways of generating, new leads, appointments and sales. So you will also see the assumptive being used very effectively in the appointment setting scripts.

Now let me get back to the back ground of the appointment setting scripts. I had given you an example of the most effective telemarketer I had ever worked with, now let me give you another example of the greatest appointment setter I have ever worked with. It was also during the same time period of the example I gave on the best telemarketer I worked with. I am currently still working with this extraordinary appointment setter. The telemarketer I mentioned before is also still employed with one of my clients as well.

How one Appointment Setter set over 5,000 appointments in one year!

Think about it for a minute? Over 5,000 appointments in one year? Now that is impressive. If you're like most of the sales people I know, you would love to have an appointment setter like that on your staff! 5,000 appointments in one year, it is a sales persons dreams. Appointments are the name of the game. Without appointments a sales person cannot sell. Without getting in front of someone it is impossible to sell.

There are two ways to get in front of people. One they come to you and the other is you go to them, but one thing is for sure, whether they come to you or you go to them, an appointment is needed.

In my eyes appointment setting is not telemarketing although it is indeed a form of telemarketing. Anyone can set appointments, but to get someone not to stand you up. To get someone to comply with your requests for them not only to meet with you but to also gather important documentation that is required to do business with them is in my opinion an art form.

I have trained appointment setters for many years and in many industries. I remember the days when I was in an industry when we could set an appointment with everyone in town. Everyone qualified for our products and services. Renters and homeowners alike, we could and would meet with everyone in town. The only criteria were that they be 18 years of age. I remember a time when we could also meet with the husband or wife. It did not matter if the other one was there or not, because of our products and services. A time when our prospect did not need to gather any type of documentation. I remember how very easy it used to be to get in front of people.

Who am I kidding? It is still easy to get in front of people. The businesses I have consulted for over the past few years are just a lot more complicated. It has been a process of having to pre-qualify prospects first and then not all prospects can qualify for our products or services. Now also in the industries I have consulted for we need a lot of documentation from prospects. We need their most recent 2 years of W'2's, one month of pay stubs, 3 months of bank statements, mortgage statement, deed of trust, copy of their note, hazard insurance information. Well, I don't need this with all industries but definitely for the mortgage industry which is one of the main industries I have consulted for. I only bring this up to give you an idea of what is needed in order to set an appointment. These are the exact appointments this extraordinary appointment setter set, and she was able to set over 5,000 of them. For a large part of the year she was the only appointment setter whose appointments supported a company of 35 employees! Not many companies can say that!

This is another reason why I would consider this to be the greatest appointment setting script in the world. Just imagine a team of 5 appointment setters setting these types of appointments and each averaging over 5,000 appointments per year. That would be over 20,000 appointments for one year for only five appointment setters.

All in all this appointment setting script has set over 100,000 appointments per year with all of the separate promotions I would run for many years for small companies. Over the past 12 years, I would say this script alone has set well over one million appointments. Keep in mind that these appointments have been with small companies and with smaller campaigns of only 8-12 appointment setters at a time. So it is not like we were setting appointments with call centers of several hundred people. If we were, we would probable have set hundreds of millions of appointments.

Proven Rebuttals that really work (Overcoming Objections)

Common Objections and overcoming them with rebuttals

Encountering objections should be expected and appreciated by all sales people. Objections are a necessary part of any sale. While some sales might have more objections than others you should expect them with all of your prospects, clients and during all of your presentations.

A great sales person is never caught off guard when these inevitable objections arise. That is because they expect them and are very prepared to use rebuttals to overcome them. A great sales person is trained in all areas of selling and using rebuttals to overcome objections is an area they have mastered well. It is the second most important thing in a sale second to the assumption. The assumption and the rebuttals work hand in hand.

With every product or service, there are really only about 10-15 objections that will come up over and over again. This is true for almost any product or service. If you are not sure what they are for your product or service, ask your sales manager if they have any material on their rebuttals or in the training manual. If they do not, don't be alarmed I will teach you how to create them from scratch. If you are wondering why I first said go to your sales manager first instead of us just creating them from scratch?

It is because we should not attempt to reinvent the wheel when ever it is not necessary. There are most likely sales people that were with your organization way before you got there. There are also most likely many sales people that have had tremendous success with your organization that sell the same products and services you will be. Typically they have already learned what the rebuttals are and have already been through the trial and error you will most likely go through so why try to reinvent the wheel when you could take a short cut and save yourself weeks, months or even years.

If they do not have any material, then you may want to approach the top 1-2-3 sales people in your organization and pick each of their brains. I can almost guarantee you that the top producer has already created some material of their own that they use. Even if they have not put it on paper, I can almost guarantee you they use a particular formula and say the exact same things. They also will know what the top 10-15 rebuttals are from their prospects.

If that does not work, then get a pen and note pad and start gathering the information for yourself. After meeting with each client, write down what where the objections each prospect said. Write it down for both the clients you sold and the clients that you lost.

Write down the objections you overcame and the objections you did not. Keep all of the results separate by client. In other words do not mix the same rebuttals down on the same page. You will not need to do this with all clients, but only about 10-15. From all of the results, look at the objection you heard of the most. Then the objection you heard second to the most and so on. Do this with the objections.

That will be the first list of the top objections and what you should expect to hear with almost all presentations. You may not hear all of them from each client, but I can almost guarantee you will hear on or two with each client.

After you have completed your objections, write down the objections you were able to overcome. Write them down on the same sheet as the objections per client. Write it on the same 10-15 clients and then also separate them in the order of the most first. In other words the objection you were able to overcome the most, followed the objection you were able to overcome the second most and so on.

With the objections you were able to over come, also write down what you said to overcome them. Also write down what you did if anything to overcome the objections.

The top 10-15 objections you overcame will be the ones you will hear on a regular basis with all clients. Again you might not have to over come all of them per client but you will have a variety of them you will need to overcome with each client.

You must learn and master the rebuttals and responses to overcome all of them. You should look at the rebuttal examples I have included in this book and try to format your rebuttals in a similar fashion. It should be in a script format. You should master the best way to say it, and the best way is the way that results in the highest ratios. Once you have done that, you will need to respond to the objections with the rebuttals the exact same way with all clients. No exceptions. So once you hear a particular objection, you will use the rebuttal that is for that objection one hundred percent of the time exactly as it is written.

Do this and I can guarantee you will start closing more sales. It depends on how committed you are by not only researching what objections to expect and which rebuttals to use, but the results from the sales people I train using rebuttals are typically double what their old results were. So I believe you to can double your current results by just implementing this easy yet affective way to respond and over come objections.

Oliver's Theory of Sales

The First Scientific Sales Formula

It has taken me the past 15 years and over 250,000 prospects and clients to create and develop the sales formula. Sales are absolutely a science and I was on a mission to create the scientific formula of sales.

Just like Einstein's Theory of Relativity, there is a mathematical formula for selling. Sales just don't happen! Sales are made by a series of processes that have a beginning, middle and end. This is a formula that has not really been defined as a scientific formula so I took it upon myself to develop the formula. So far this has been a challenging task. Although I am one of the masters of sales in our Country and I know exactly what the sales formula is, it has been challenging to say the least to be able to put it into a mathematical equation or an actual formula. I am not a physicist like Sir Isaac Newton or Albert Einstein, but then again, I'm sure they couldn't sell like me either.

This is my disclosure to announce that I have indeed created the scientific formula of sales but it is a work in progress.

I'm going to search for the brightest mathematical minds on the planet to help me finalize on the scientific formula of sales. I will at least give you my first version of it until I can develop the finalized masterpiece.

I encourage all who read this to give it some serious thought and to see if you can create a better sales formula. I am always open to any and all suggestions so all who dare to make history, I welcome your insight!

Oliver's Theory of Sales

To all sales there is a process and elements involved with a sale. A sale does not grow on trees, nor does it rise from the East or set in the west. A sale does not just happen. Just like there is a particular formula and elements for vaccines, so is there a formula and elements for sales. A vaccine does not just happen, science has developed it and created the formula and if we are to create a formula for sales we must also understand that sales are in fact a science.

Oliver's Sales Formula

$$S = (EM)\ IP\ (EM + DCA) + ESP\ (AO + O^2) + AC$$

Before a sale can be made there must be some elements and factors that need to all be present.

There must be **(EM)** Effective Marketing which will equal (=) an **(IP)** Identified Prospect plus along with **(EM)** Effective Marketing with the (Identified Prospect) plus **(+)** **(DCA)** Direct Contact Appointment plus **(+)** an **(ESP)** Effective Sales Presentation along with **(AO)** Anticipated Objections plus **(+)** **(OO)** Overcoming Objections is the sum **(+)** of the **(AC)** Assumptive Close **(Sale)**.

Of course there will also be several other elements and factors that will be in addition to the elements and factors which will be covered in great detail in a later edition or in sales seminars. For now I just wanted to introduce the world to Oliver's Theory of Sales!

$$S = (EM)\ IP\ (EM + DCA) + ESP\ (AO + O^2) + AC$$

If we take out the common aspects of the sale; such as the identified prospect which we all know you must have and goes without saying, along with the effective marketing which we also know you need to have direct contact which is also a given and then of course objections and overcoming objections is technically a part of the presentation you would end up with this sales formula.

$$S = IP + ESP + AC$$
$S = IP + ESP + AC$, which says that a sale equals an identified prospect plus an effective sales presentation plus the assumptive close.

You can do it!

I'd like to finish by reminding you that "You Can Do It"!

What ever it is for you, you can do it. Don't let anything or anyone stop you. Don't allow anyone to discourage you. I can assure you that it will not be easy. If it was easy, everyone would have what you want, but it is not easy and you should be glad that it's not. That is the only sure way to know that you will be able to get everything and anything that you want. Know that most other people will quite well before even attempting to do anything to get what they want. You are already well on your way. You've bought this book! You are improving on yourself right now. You have already taken some action in pursuit of your dreams and you can do it!

Know that almost everyone you know and even many who you don't know are going to try to deter you from your goals. For some reason they think they have to protect you. Others may also be jealous that they never attempted to reach any of their goals and they would hate to see someone else reach their goals and prove they made a mistake. They would rather you fail or not even attempt it, so they can feel better about themselves. For whatever reason anyone tried to deter you from your dreams and goals, do not allow them to.

If you're not sure you can handle all the ridicule, rejection, objection and concerns of everyone else. You may want to consider not mentioning your objectives with others.

If you're strong enough to deal with the constant negative criticism and you know it will not interfere with your goals and dreams, then by all means tell the world what you are going to accomplish! That's how I do it.

I announce it to my peers, friends, family and acquaintances before I really even know how I'm going to do it. I just know that I know I can do anything I set my mind to do, and that is one of the ways that motivate me to do it. When I announce it to everyone, I know they are going to hold me accountable by telling asking me the next time they see me if I've achieved my objectives? I also know that they are not asking out of excitement, but hoping I say I haven't done anything or I haven't had any success, because they are ready to tell me how they told me so. Even in situations when I have not achieved the level I had wanted, I know that is part of getting to my final destination and I know that when they tell me how they told me so or how I will fail or how I'm expecting too much, I just have to keep on keeping on so I can tell them I told you I would do it!

Oliver P. Maldonado

You must believe in yourself and know that you are going to reach your final destination if you don't give up. You can do it! Anthony Robbins uses a great example in his amazing book "Awaken the Giant Within", if you haven't read it yet, I would strongly recommend you pick up a copy it will change your life for ever. But in his book he uses an example how an airplane if of course over 90% of the time, yet it always seems to reach its destination! That is a great example, think about it. If the pilot got discouraged and said, I'm off course, we'll never get there, they in fact will never get to their destination and their thoughts would actually control their actions which would have dire consequences! Don't be discouraged when you've tried something and it hasn't worked, it is okay, you just have to know that you'll now have to try a different approach. And when that approach does not work, then try yet another approach. When that one doesn't work, then again try another approach. Keep changing and adapting your approach until you reach your final destination. I can assure you that if you continue changing your approach and not give up you in fact will reach your goals and dreams. That I can guarantee you!

Contacting the author

The author Oliver P. Maldonado can be retained to consult with your organization to help train your sales and marketing staff. Oliver P. Maldonado is an expert in sales & marketing and is one of the most sought after Sales consultants in the industry.

Oliver P. Maldonado is also available for speaking engagements.

You can contact the author several different ways. The first is you can call the publishing company Author First at **1-800-839-8640** and they can get you in touch with the author. They can also help coordinate speaking engagements along with book signings.

You can also get additional information by visiting the authors website at WWW.OliverMaldonado.com

WWW.TheGreatestSalesbookintheWorld.com

Contracting the author to train your sales staff

Oliver P. Maldonado is a sales trainer and sales consultant can be contracted to consult with your sales and marketing staff to increase your lead generation, referrals or new business production which will increase the overall production in your organization. What ever your needs and desires are Oliver P. Maldonado can help increase the weekly, monthly and yearly production.

Oliver P. Maldonado has consulted and generated very successful sales and marketing campaigns for many industries. Industries such as the Mortgage Industry, Real Estate, Satellite Dish, Financial

Planning, Insurance, Home and Business Alarm Systems, Cellular phone and the Health & Fitness industry to mention just a few.

If you are serious about increasing your companies sales & growing your company! You will need to generate new business and sales for your company.

If you are serious about generating new business and sales for your organization? You should be working with Oliver P. Maldonado

WWW.OliverMaldonado.com

TheGreatestSalesbookintheWorld.com

About the Author

Oliver Maldonado has spent the past 12 years mastering the Art of Sales. He has traveled around the country consulting with companies and training salespeople. In his entire career he has been able to maintain a closing ratio above 90%. Oliver has trained regular people and converted them into great salespeople. His sales forces have all maintained a combined closing ratio of over 75%, right from the start.